Leadership is a lifelong jou⋯⋯⋯⋯⋯⋯'e are
people like Lisa Potter wh⋯⋯⋯⋯⋯⋯urney
that serve as maps. If you're ⋯⋯⋯⋯⋯⋯ your
leadership to the next level, this book will help you do just that. If you want to grow
higher, you must go deeper!

—Mark Batterson
New York Times best-selling author of *The Circle Maker*
Lead Pastor, National Community Church, Washington, DC

There are a lot of leadership books out there, but *The Collective Journey* is a powerful
leadership tool for female leaders. By examining core-self, the power of story, calling,
and community, Lisa creates a process to have a sustainable leadership pipeline for
future women leaders.

—Scott Wilson
Author, *IMPACT: Releasing the Power of Influence*
Founder, 415leaders.com and RSGleaders.com

When Lisa Potter speaks, I like to listen. She is intelligent, competent, articulate,
passionate about spurring on needed change in people and institutions, and sensi-
tive to the Spirit. When you apply that package to an important topic like healthy
living and leadership for Christian women, you end up with a book you don't want
to miss. I guarantee it'll make you think, and ultimately, it will lead you to delve
deeper in relationships to make your dreams become a reality.

—Dr. Carolyn Tennant
Speaker, Mentor, Professor
Author of *Catch the Wind of the Spirit* and *Keys to the Apostolic and Prophetic*

I don't know many people more passionate about equipping and empowering
women to find their place and their voice than Lisa Potter. I'm so excited about *The
Collective Journey* and how many women are going to discover their full potential
through the inspirational AND practical content that she offers through it.

—Lora Batterson
National Community Church, Washington, DC

The Collective Journey is about far more than collecting a group of friends together
for leadership development. It is about collecting your whole self (life experiences,
memories, encounters with God) and bringing it all to the foot of Jesus for evaluation and reinterpretation. It is about a God-given redemptive perspective that

helps boost you toward the divine objectives. This study is for you if you are ready to go to the next level in your faith.

—Pastor Marlyn DeFoggi
West End Assembly of God, Richmond, Virginia

Lisa clearly understands the power of community for women who want to fulfill God's calling on their lives. *The Collective Journey* provides a clear framework to help us encourage one another to pursue life-giving soul care, understand our unique design, and step into our God-given purpose. I'm so grateful for this beautiful resource!

—Kerry Clarensau
Author, *Secrets, Redeemed, Fully His* and *A Beautiful Life*
Camas, Washington

The apostle Paul writes in 1 Corinthians 12:7 (NIV), "Now to EACH ONE (emphasis mine) the manifestation of the Spirit is given for the common good." This is inclusive of men and women from every tribe, tongue, language, and nation. Then, beyond the nine spiritual gifts, Paul goes on to mention apostles, prophets, teachers, workers of miracles, healers, helpers, administrators, and tongue-speakers without making any disqualifications. The Spirit gives them to "each one." Lisa Potter is an advocate for and mentor of women to help them find their callings and gifts and then opens doors for them to serve in God's kingdom. Her voice, through *The Collective Journey*, truly serves the "common good."

—Harvey A. Herman
Chi Alpha Campus Ministries, Missionary

The Collective Journey is not just a book. It is a life-changing invitation to a new way of living—a journey, indeed, of spiritual depth in an otherwise shallow world. Lisa's passionate voice for the Lord is heard throughout keeping the reader eager for the next page. I know Lisa as a colleague, a leader, a teacher, and now, as an author. Her message needs to be everyone's message. I highly commend *The Collective Journey* to you.

—Dr. Robert J. Rhoden
President, Ascent College

Most people pack their bags when preparing for a journey, but this one is different. In *The Collective Journey*, Lisa lovingly invites you to *unpack* your bags to make room for the treasures you will discover along the way. This journey is a transformational one that will call you to take a seat at a table where communion and community begin. Are you ready for your life and leadership to be revolutionized? Come to the table!

—Stacy Eubanks
AGWM Missionary

As a young woman just starting out in life, I craved a deeper walk with Jesus. I needed a structured discipleship pathway to lead me into a God-ordained life. Thankfully, women leaders in my church reached out to me and mentored me. But, Oh! how I wish we'd had *The Collective Journey*! It speaks to every part of our lives, connecting mature leaders to women who long to grow and lead through an authentically spiritual and healthy life in Jesus. Lisa Potter provides a life-impacting resource that fills a need in the lives of women in the local church and beyond. Both practical and deeply spiritual, *The Collective Journey* provides a biblical pathway for growing in Jesus while journeying together, something we all long for in today's busy, fragmented world.

—Kay Burnett
National Director of Women's Ministries for the Assemblies of God
Credentialed Minister, Church Planter

When Lisa and I first met in seminary, I knew she was a kindred spirit. We share a deep passion to invite leaders into personal wholeness. *The Collective Journey* is not just another tired, "How-to lead like a CEO" leadership book; it invites leaders into something much more compelling, integrated, life-giving, and sacred.

With personal candor and stark vulnerability, Lisa leads us through her story of "living through the pain of high expectations, loneliness, criticism, and spiritual and physical exhaustion," into a comprehensive and transformative journey that brings flourishing to our life, leadership, and to those we serve.

Lisa doesn't let us short-circuit the pathway to wholeness or leave us languishing in theory. She does, however, with clarity, powerful analogies, profound insights, and rich exegesis, offer us a way of leadership seeped in both personal and communal practices. In fact, intensely practical, each area of focus requires real-life engagement in spiritual retreat, personality assessment, story-mapping, journaling, forgiveness, remembrance, care of the body, and so much more.

As I read *The Collective Journey*, I found myself whispering, "I wish I could have been part of a Journey Collective when I was a younger leader." So, don't wait. This book, this journey, is for you now! I anticipate *The Collective Journey* will become an essential resource for female leaders for years to come. May it be so.

—Dr. Gail Johnsen
Author of *All There: How Attentiveness Shapes Authentic Leadership*

Amid the shift happening within the church, God has raised Lisa Potter as a mother among God's people for this time. God is cultivating the next generation of female leaders deep within to prepare and sustain the church for the days ahead. *The Collective Journey* will serve as a much-needed companion alongside any woman on her ministry pilgrimage.

—Dr. Stephanie Nance
Adult Spiritual Formation Pastor
Chapel Springs Church

The Collective Journey is inspirational and practical. The call to journey to your mountain where God awaits is one of sorrow and pain, laughter and joy, and disappointment and dreaming. Lisa shines light on the path to God, self, and community. A must-read for women ready to step into their leadership calling and own the responsibility to bring the next generation with them.

—Dr. John Battaglia
Doctor of Ministry, Program Director, at the
Assemblies of God Theological Seminary
Capitol Commission Chaplain to the Missouri Legislature

The Collective Journey emphasizes two vitally important truths. First, life is a journey. God is calling us to become more than we are today. Second, no one should take that journey alone. Lisa Potter gives practical strategies for moving forward and connecting with others. We are called to plant our feet on higher ground. Lisa helps us get there.

—Scott Young
Pastor, Church of Hope
Sarasota, Florida

Lisa Potter is a beautiful example of a leader deeply valuing a previously unmet need and, with no excuses, creating a relational experience that shepherds the soul of women to an awareness of the presence of God in real life. *The Collective Journey* will guide you through some intentional steps that will be golden in discovering gifts and calling. Lisa is a community builder, so you better believe that this book will embolden you to engage others and deepen your journey in the context of relationships.

—Noemi Chavez
Pastor, Revive Church
Cofounder of Brave Global

For foreign and subsidiary rights, contact the author.

Cover design by: Sara Young

ISBN: 978-1-957369-02-0   1 2 3 4 5 6 7 8 9 10

Printed in the United States of America

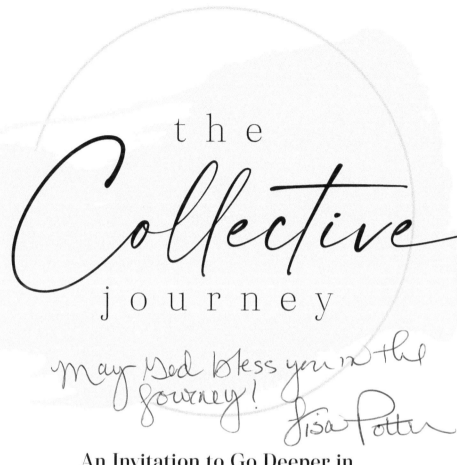

the *Collective* journey

May God bless you in the journey!
Lisa Potter

An Invitation to Go Deeper in Your Life and Leadership

LISA POTTER

ARROWS & STONES

DEDICATION

*To my husband, Frank—you
wildly cheer for me and all women
to step into their leadership calling.
I am the leader I am today because of you.*

ACKNOWLEDGMENTS

It took a lot of prayer, high fives, encouragement, and, "You go, girl"s for me to complete this writing journey. I knew in my heart that *The Collective Journey* would be a book one day, but at the same time, I doubted this time would ever come.

In the middle of my dreams to publish the book, my father passed away. The time I invested in him during the last few months of his journey on this earth was worth the wait of a published book. Although he is not here with me now, I know he is cheering me on from the other side.

To all of you who came alongside me in some way, you are a part of *The Collective Journey* story, but more importantly, you are a part of my story, and I am blessed to count you as dear friends.

To my husband and family, I love you, Frank, Lindsay, Andrew, and Allison. You are my number one cheerleaders.

To my mom, you listened and prayed, as always, and I am overwhelmed with goodness that I get the privilege of being your daughter.

To my first friends Ann and Naomi, you pulled me out of my depression and helped me see the possibilities of community, and I am forever grateful.

To Jodi Detrick, a kindred heart, forever friend, constant cheerleader, and coach, you are a true-blue Jesus-hearted woman. Without your direction and insight, *The Collective Journey* may not have become a reality. Thank you, my friend, for believing in me.

To my first Collective Journey group, an academic field test that turned quickly to friendship, it doesn't seem right not to mention you by name: Lindsay Potter, Julia Putprush, Victoria Davis, Kelsey Bradley, Kayla Fuoco, Carla Bailey, Shauna Nicholson, Stacy Eubanks, Natalie Hill, Rochelle Roman, Kelli Ferguson, Julia Mockabee, Wendi Rawls, Hannah Horst, Jessica Crews, and Courtney Barnes. You are world-changers, and I am cheering you on wildly with high fives and, "You go, girl!"s.

To Marlyn DeFoggi and the women of West End Assembly of God, I so appreciate your going on *The Collective Journey* and proving that women in all seasons of life and leadership need what is in the pages of this book.

To Dr. Cheryl Taylor, for asking me if I have ever thought about furthering my education and then making me feel that anything is possible, I owe my education journey to your obedience to ask the question.

To Erica Huinda, my editor, who makes me sound much smarter than I really am, you are an absolute grammar gem and wordsmith.

To the Potomac Ministry Network Executive Team, AGTS (Assemblies of God Theological Seminary), and the professors, thank you for coming alongside me and believing in my heart and passion to mentor the next generation of female leaders.

To Kay Burnett, you read the academic manuscript and then engaged me in a way to make my heart's passion a reality. I love and appreciate your leadership. You truly are an amazing cheerleader.

Thank you Martijn van Tilborgh, Rick Edwards, Four Rivers Media Publishing, and the amazing publishing team for making this book a reality and making me feel like my words were important, useful, and can serve a greater purpose.

And finally, but most importantly, to my Lord and Savior, Jesus Christ, who redeems our lives and makes them beautiful and useful with kingdom purpose, I daily whisper the words written in 2 Thessalonians 1:11 (MSG): "We pray for you all the time—pray that our God will make you fit for what he's called you to be, pray that he'll fill your good ideas and acts of faith with his own energy so that it all amounts to something."

For this, I am grateful.

FOREWORD

Once in a while, holy favor and some mysterious grace pulls back the curtain to allow us glimpses of someone else's embryonic (but already sparkling-with-promise) God-dream in formation. That happened for me over several years of heart-deep conversations with my dear friend and ministry colleague, Lisa Potter. The pain, frustration, and sense of aloneness from Lisa's own early ministry experiences birthed a passion to find a relational, doable, reproducible way to ensure those coming behind her have an entirely different ministry experience, one that is healthy, supported, and infused with sound biblical patterns that sustain leaders for the long haul.

Can I just tell you, what I saw back then stirred new hope in my heart, especially for a younger generation of sisters in ministry leadership who are desperate for wise, accessible mentorship and where-the-rubber-meets-the-road resources for the daring journey ahead. Lisa poured years of intense study, prayer, and research (not to mention blood, sweat, and tears) into this God-directed passion. She gleaned from decades of ministry experience, her own and that of trusted colleagues and advisors. And what I see *now* that Lisa's dream is fully formed, contained in the pages of this beautiful book, and already infusing lives with courage for those vital next steps. . . well, this takes my breath away!

The Collective Journey is for every woman who is determined to keep saying *yes* to Jesus and His calling to serve and lead with a bold, anointed humility. It is for each woman who wants to make sure other called women are encouraged, supported, and resourced for their own journey of ministry leadership. It is for groups of women who long for a community of sisters who *get* each other and are committed to travel together, sharing each other's stories and strengths in the presence of Jesus.

Here's the thing. You were never meant to walk the path of ministry alone, dear called sister. There is so much help and hope waiting for you in the pages ahead, and I cannot remember being more excited about the unveiling of a new book. It is with conviction and celebration that I say, *The Collective Journey* by my amazing friend and authentic, gifted ministry leader extraordinaire, Lisa Potter, is for YOU! Grab a cup of coffee and a friend's hand—it's time for your journey to begin!

Jodi Detrick
North Bend, Washington
Author, *The Jesus-Hearted Woman* and *The Settled Soul*

CONTENTS

INTRODUCTION

This book is about journeys—collective journeys and individual journeys. It comes from deep places birthed through my personal pain and passions as a female leader, wife, mother, daughter, sister, friend, and mentor.

This book is about journeys–collective journeys and individual journeys.

My lack of a mentor in the early years of my life and leadership journey compels me to mentor the next generation of female leaders. While living through the pain of high expectations, loneliness, criticism, and spiritual and physical exhaustion, my life journey became a lesson called "Things I Wish I Had Known."

I learned early on that I cannot take my health and wholeness journey alone as a leader. I needed a community, a collective group of women, that would walk with me through the process of becoming a better version of myself. Born out of this necessary kinship ensued *The Collective Journey*. What you hold in your hands is a book for a personal journey, and a relational mentoring model developed to effectively engage younger female leaders in a journey toward transformation and wholeness.

The personal, biblical, and professional research guided me to several lessons:

- The importance of taking care of the soul.
- The power of story.
- The need to know my calling.
- The necessity of developing a community of support and friendships.

Ultimately, I also learned that effective life and leadership journeys recognize the importance of creating a sustainable pipeline for the next generation. The key strategies required for wholeness are mentoring and building relational communities.

The Four Foundations

The Collective Journey is a relational mentoring model developed to effectively engage younger female leaders in a journey toward transformation and wholeness. It utilizes the four primary foundations found in the Paul and Timothy leadership mentoring model in 2 Timothy 1:1-18 and employs four primary elements discovered in the passage: core-self (the power of inward reflection), communion (the power of story), calling (the power of God's design in you), and community (the power of a network).

The four foundations of life and leadership are characterized by either an inward focus or outer focus, both of which remain important. In his book *Soul Keeping,* John Ortberg explains the difference between the inward and outward life: "We each have an outer life and inner one. My outer self is the public, visible me. My accomplishments, my work, and my reputation lie there. My inner life is where my secret thoughts and hopes and wishes live. Because my inner life is invisible, it is easy to neglect. No one has direct access to it, so it wins no applause."[1] All four foundational elements work together to bring the awareness that wholeness of life flows from the inside, the part of the individual not on display.

The scriptural reference in Paul's second letter to Timothy, "a son of the faith," gives a timeless example of the importance of mentoring and passing the baton to the next generation, creating a leadership pipeline. Although written in a patriarchal society, the Bible translates well into today's culture, showing that God calls men and women to lead.

The writing of 2 Timothy remains extraordinarily personal and gives the sense of a spiritual father recounting his last wishes and advice to a spiritual son. In the personal nature of the book, Paul shares memories, values generational continuity in

---

1 John Ortberg, *Soul Keeping: Caring for the Most Important Part of You* (Grand Rapids, MI: Zondervan, 2014), 38.

serving God, gives reminders and encouragement to remain strong in the faith and endure suffering, reiterates the church policies against false teaching, and encourages Timothy to "preach the word" (2 Timothy 4:2).

Paul concludes the letter by expressing his immediate needs as life for him will soon end. In essence, the book is the last will, which reminds Timothy of all that Paul has taught him. It passes the baton of leadership to the next generation. Second Timothy stands as a tribute to Paul's legacy and an urgent reminder to remain faithful to the gospel and continue the ministry Paul started for future generations.

In this biblical evidence, we see that God calls leaders to finish well and multiply. The Paul and Timothy model confirms the necessity of spiritual fathers and mothers raising up sons and daughters of the faith.

As we read 2 Timothy 1:1-18, the connection to the four foundations of core-self, communion, calling, and community emerge and solidify "The Things I Wish I Had Known."

Paul reminds Timothy (and us), "Guard the good deposit that was entrusted to you—guard it with the help of the Holy Spirit who lives in us" (2 Timothy 1:14). The first foundation, core-self, the power of inward reflection, begins the journey toward a healthier inner you. Safeguard your heart, your inner self, because from this place flows the most essential part of you—your true self. It cannot be hidden. If the soul is unhealthy, it will eventually peak through in unhealthy habits and places of our life and leadership. The second inner-focused foundation is communion, the power of your story. The practice of the communion sacrament brings a powerful analogy to how we can embrace the power of our story as seen through God's story—His death, burial, and resurrection. Together we consider the practice of remembering, forgiveness, and gratitude.

The reminder for Timothy's story appears early on in 2 Timothy 1:3-5, where Paul is mentoring his son in the faith. He urges Timothy to remember where he has come from. The power and goodness of faith that first lived in the heart of his grandmother Lois and in his mother, Eunice. Timothy's story shaped his life and leadership.

Next, there is the outward focus of calling, the power of God's design in you. This foundation builds upon the revelations of the inner focus of core-self and communion. So it is with an earnestness that Paul reminds Timothy, "to fan into flame the gift of God, which is in you through the laying on of my hands. For the Spirit

God gave us does not make us timid, but gives us power, love, and self-discipline" (2 Timothy 1:6-7).

Paul reminds Timothy to walk in his individual calling and fan it into a flame. To not let the brightness that only he can bring be extinguished because he is fearful and timid. Find that place of your calling and walk in it—meaning and passions.

The last foundation, community, the power of a network, is rooted in the number one struggle for women—loneliness. Paul experiences the aloneness of life and leadership as he writes his letter to Timothy, reminding him to remember the people who stand with you:

> You know that everyone in the province of Asia has deserted me, including Phygelus and Hermogenes. May the Lord show mercy to the household of Onesiphorus because he often refreshed me and was not ashamed of my chains.
> —2 Timothy 1:15-16

This can be seen in his writing to Timothy: reminding him of his roots, illustrating the power of story, emphasizing his calling and the rekindling of the gift of God, guarding deposits, and standing with those who will be there until the end. Perhaps we should ask ourselves the same question Paul was probably thinking when he wrote his second letter to Timothy, *If I am not here, who will do what I have been doing?*

The Necessity for Transformation and Wholeness

God calls leaders to finish well and multiply. The Paul and Timothy model confirms that the spiritual leader's job is to recognize the calling in others and help those individuals go from where they are to where God intends for them to be.

Whether you embark on *The Collective Journey* individually or as a mentor and mentee, both hold the significant task of developing and maturing leadership:

> When Christ calls leaders to Christian ministry He intends to develop them to their full potential. Each of us in leadership is responsible to continue developing in accordance with God's processing all our life. Unless we experience God's ongoing development, we will not be able to help others develop their leadership capacity.[2]

---

2 Randy D. Reese and Robert Loane, *Deep Mentoring: Guiding Others on Their Leadership Journey* (Downers Grove, IL: InterVarsity Press, 2012), 146.

When we take the journey to grow into maturity and fulfill the calling God has on our lives, reciprocal mentoring will undoubtedly occur. The call to maturity and continued development remains crucial to our personal wholeness in life and leadership, profoundly impacting the ability to live and lead well and ultimately lead the generation coming from behind. In addition, reciprocal mentoring creates a pipeline and abundance of leaders in the field.

Sheryl Sandberg, chief operating officer of Facebook, notes the positive power of reciprocal mentor/mentee relationships:

Sociologists and psychologists have long observed our deep desire to participate in reciprocal behavior. The fact that humans feel obligated to return favors has been documented in virtually all societies and underpins all kinds of social relationships. The mentor/mentee relationship is no exception. When done right, everybody flourishes.[3]

Sandberg also believes that "peers can also mentor and sponsor one another."[4] The objective of mentor/mentee relationships centers on cultivating a culture of cascading relationships, in which individuals take responsibility for both their own and others' health and wholeness.

Though mentoring relationships and creating leadership pipelines remain essential for building the church and spreading the gospel, barriers often exist when it comes to implementing such tools for women, especially as it pertains to the church and workplace. When ministry or leadership teams form, individual group members bring their own cultural biases, norms, values, customs, historical narratives, and behavioral patterns.

When ministry or leadership teams form, individual group members bring their own cultural biases, norms, values, customs, historical narratives, and behavioral patterns.

---

3 Sheryl Sandberg, *Lean In: Women, Work, and the Will to Lead* (New York: Alfred A. Knopf, 2013), 69.
4 Sandberg, *Lean In*, 74.

Further, as it pertains to women and men in a given environment, individuals may differ on what they deem "natural" for the roles of men and women. Questions can help reveal various factors that influence how one views gender roles: How did your father view women in leadership? How did your mother view women in leadership? Did you see women actively taking leadership roles in your church or community? Differing answers to these questions often result in different viewpoints on the roles of men and women in society.

In her article titled "What Happens When We See Women Teach the Bible," Sharon Hodde Miller explains what happened to her:

> As a college student, I was confused about the church. Women mostly occupied administrative positions. Even in my college parachurch organization, we rarely had a woman speak. Given the scarcity of female role models, I wasn't sure where to turn.[5]

She notes that it was not until she attended a Passion conference in Atlanta where Beth Moore took the stage and "spoke with power, competency, conviction, and most of all, anointing" that she realized her own potential and calling.[6] After that experience, Sharon started her journey to earn a master of divinity and PhD to equip herself for writing and speaking.

Lori O'Dea concurs with the idea that women must model leadership to others. While Lori was preaching at a girls' retreat, a counselor asked a little girl who was crying at the altar how she could pray for her. The child replied that she was simply overwhelmed with the fact that God would call girls. O'Dea makes her point: "Experience imprints indelible lessons. If people do not have the opportunity to experience a woman's leadership, they will likely avoid it, or worse, condemn it."[7] Mentoring a next generation of female leaders will open the flow in the pipeline for women in leadership, helping to change cultural norms and break down biases that hinder women. Having more female leaders will create health and wholeness in life and leadership.

The multinational firm KPMG issued their *Women's Leadership Study*, which reveals concrete conclusions supporting the benefits of early mentoring for women:

5 Sharon Hodde Miller, "What Happens When We See Women Teach the Bible," *Christianity Today*, http://www.christianitytoday.com/women/2015/january/what-happens-when-we-see-women-teach-bible.html.

6 Miller, "What Happens."

7 Lori O'Dea, "Is Leadership a Gender-Neutral Issue?" *Influence Magazine*, August-September 2015, 46.

A woman's perception of leadership begins not with collegiate academic success, her first big break, or when she's named to a position of power. The trajectory to female leadership starts much earlier and is defined by key influences throughout life.[8]

The study identified several key components for developing and creating a pipeline of the next generation of female leaders, including: "how these women were socialized to leadership growing up; explore their self-perceptions growing up and today; uncover which characteristics are associated with leadership; examine who influenced these women in learning about applying business leadership; and discover concrete ways to help more women move forward into leadership roles."[9]

The study further envisions the need for the awareness and development of female leaders to begin early in young girls:

Imagine a young girl—perhaps a daughter, a niece or the girl down the street. She is smart. She is ambitious. She believes in herself and her abilities. From a young age, she has a desire to lead—to inspire others to greatness, to surpass expectations, to better the world. Yet as she grows up, two elements will affect her ability to lead: confidence and connections. Throughout her life, she either will receive what she needs to build these two key components of leadership—or she won't.[10]

Women want to be successful in life and leadership, but something often holds them back. Developing young girls and training other women to mentor and serve as role models remain imperative for creating the next-generation female leader's pipeline. Leadership does not stand alone; a path to leadership development must exist. Healthy and whole leaders experience guidance along the way.

Healthy and whole leaders experience
guidance along the way.

---

8 KPMG, *Women's Leadership Study*, "Moving Women Forward into Leadership Roles," https://home.kpmg/content/dam/kpmg/ph/pdf/ThoughtLeadershipPublications/KPMGWomensLeadershipStudy.pdf.

9 KPMG, *Women's Leadership Study*.

10 KPMG, *Women's Leadership Study*.

Factors such as these four foundations improve health and wholeness in life and leadership: personal leadership development, the power of story, skill sets, and the power of a network.

Women grow stronger through being together; this proves especially true when women connect intergenerationally and learn from one another. Closing the gaps in generational leadership relies on successfully passing the baton of leadership. However, if the baton drops, gaps will appear in leadership, and women will suffer from a lack of leadership development. Identifying and mentoring female leaders who are satisfied in their calling, belong to a meaningful community, share their stories to create change, and seek leadership development will enhance the pipeline with strong, capable female leaders.

CHAPTER 1
THE NECESSARY JOURNEY

I look up to the mountains; does my strength come from mountains? No, my strength comes from God, who made heaven, and earth, and mountains.
—Psalm 121: 1-2 (MSG)

I always feel like I'm in over my head or between a rock and a hard place. Let's face it; I'm an enneagram three (overachiever). I like to tell myself that the four wing of my enneagram three gives me a much softer and more balanced side, but I'm always trying to balance the need to do more and be more.

The search for balance has made necessary journeys a part of my life and leadership. What do I mean by that phrase, *necessary journeys*? It is the *required to be done* journey. Fortunately, I get that because my enneagram number three causes me to love a to-do list.

The search for balance has made necessary journeys a part of my life and leadership.

The realm of perfection gains momentum as I begin checking off items on the list. The perfect dream becomes blissfully sweet as the accomplishments of the day soar. Then, I am back to reality where the list is longer than I imagine, the over-commitment is real, and the need for balance is something only God can curtail through the path of *necessary journeys*.

In 2012, my husband, Frank, was elected to a new leadership role that required us to leave our lead pastor role at a church we loved dearly for twenty years. The transition remained hard for me. I worked as a staff pastor leading worship, musicals, writing, casting vision for the women, and raising two children in a community we called home.

When we moved from our home of twenty years and all the memories, it would prove difficult for me to transition in the new season. I quickly erased every meeting from my calendar. I realized in the days ahead that closely tied to my identity was what I was doing. I would ask the questions, "If I am not leading worship on Sundays, then who am I?" I was addicted to the praise of people saying, "Good job!"

I had gone through other necessary journeys in my life when I battled depression for several years, but this was different. I knew that I was about to head down another path that would take me to a place where God would require emptying me—a complete trust like nothing else I had ever gone through.

As I tried to settle into our new home, the empty nest (our youngest had graduated from college weeks before), the loss of a job/ministry that I loved, and a new community, I could feel myself spiraling down. But this journey was different than before. It were as if I knew where the hike up the mountain was going to take me. I could hear the whisperings of the Holy Spirit reminding me that it was *necessary* for the ascent up the mountain.

About ten months after our move, our son got married. After looking through the photos, I noticed that my neck looked larger than usual. I thought, *Why have I not noticed this earlier?* During my self-examination, I realized that I could feel something significant that should not be there.

The following months led to doctors' visits, ultrasounds, and biopsies. I was told that I had eight tumors attached to my thyroid. One was the size of a golf ball. We discovered that the biopsy came back clear, with no sign of cancer, so I did not need surgery. But, still, I had a nagging deep inside that something was not well. I reached out to an endocrinologist and discovered that both paternal and maternal grandmothers had goiters on their thyroid and had to have surgeries. We decided that it would be better to surgically remove the tumors and the entire thyroid sooner than later with the family history.

When I went back for my follow-up visit with the surgeon, I felt good about the surgery. I thought he would look at the incision, and I would be on my way. Instead, when the surgeon entered the room, he said, "Do you want the good news or the bad news first?" I was stunned and thinking, *What bad news could there possibly be?* He would go on to tell me that I had cancer (that was the bad news). The good news was that I had made the right decision to follow my gut, seek a second opinion, and have the surgery. The fine needle biopsies tested the large tumor, but the surgical biopsy revealed cancer in the thyroid, not the tumors.

A month after the thyroid surgery, I would spend Christmas with our family at my parents' house. Little did we know that a little more than six months later, on July 1, 2014, my oldest brother would die tragically in India while hiking the Himalayan Mountains to share the gospel with unreached people groups. Later, in September of 2018, cancer showed up again in my breast after a routine exam. Although the prognosis is good, and God is faithful in every journey, my continued life is full of testing, medicine, and oncologist visits.

Unfortunately, *necessary journeys* have not been blissful or dream-perfect for me. With the two cancer diagnoses, grief, transitions, and a journey with depression, it leaves me wondering how many more *required to be done* journeys I will need to hike.

I have learned that the spiritual formation that occurs in the *necessary journeys* allows the dependency on self and others to dissipate, leading us to look upon the only source whom we can truly depend on—God. During this time of *necessary journeys*, a deeper and richer understanding of God occurs in our hearts.

During this time of **necessary journeys**,
a deeper and richer understanding
of God occurs in our hearts.

In thinking about literal mountains, like the one my brother died on in India, I must address spiritual mountains on the *need to be done journey*. The spiritual mountains we climb bring hope and faith in the hard places. Psalms 120 through 134 consist of the Psalms of Ascent. Worshipers sang the Songs of Ascent as they made their journey to Jerusalem each year for the annual feast. It was their *necessary journey.*

In the Old Testament Jewish tradition, the ritual of singing Songs of Ascent on the long passage to Jerusalem symbolizes nearness to God: feast, sacrifices, the ark of the covenant, and the holy of holies. As they left the desert of Egypt, it was an uphill climb to the city of Jerusalem, and they would sing.

Their necessary journey of ascent would entail the song of Psalm 121:

> *I lift up my eyes to the mountains—*
> *where does my help come from?*
> *My help comes from the LORD,*
> *the Maker of heaven and earth.*
> *He will not let your foot slip—*
> *he who watches over you will not slumber;*
> *indeed, he who watches over Israel*
> *will neither slumber nor sleep.*
> *The LORD watches over you—*
> *the Lord is your shade at your right hand;*
> *the sun will not harm you by day,*
> *nor the moon by night.*
> *The LORD will keep you from all harm—*
> *he will watch over your life;*
> *the LORD will watch over your coming and going*
> *both now and forevermore.*

So, my friend, as we embark on *necessary journeys,* we remind ourselves, "I look up to the mountains; does my strength come from mountains? No, my strength comes from God, who made heaven, and earth, and mountains" (Psalm 121:1-2, MSG).

Reflection Questions:

1) Can you recognize necessary journeys that you have taken?

2) What holds you back from embarking on necessary journeys?

3) What excites you about the journey?

CHAPTER 2

GOD WAITS FOR YOU
AT YOUR MOUNTAIN

Don't be afraid, I've redeemed you. I've called your name. You're mine.
When you're in over your head, I'll be there with you. When you're in rough
waters, you will not go down. When you're between a rock and a hard
place, it won't be a dead end—because I am God, your personal God.
—Isaiah 43:1-3 (MSG)

S everal years ago, I attended a prayer retreat for women leaders. At the end of the opening session, the director encouraged us to find a place for contemplative prayer and listening. I'm a floor sitter—I feel closer to God when I am closer to the ground. I sat on the floor for a long time while simply listening, tuning my heart and ears to hear what the Spirit seemed to impress on me for that moment.

It appeared as if a long time passed when I felt impressed to pick up my Bible, journal, and pen. I could tell that the Spirit wanted to share a message.

As I listened, I turned to Psalm 68:11, a new scripture for me: "The Lord announces the word and the women who proclaim it are a mighty throng."[11] I thought, *Where has this scripture been all my life?* What happened next remains significant to my purpose and calling. In my prayerful listening, I heard, *God is preparing*

---

11 All Scripture quotations, unless otherwise stated, are from the New International Version.

a mighty army of women who are full of the Spirit: warriors, prophetic voices, worshipers, trumpeters, grace-givers, bridge-builders, joy-givers, restorers of hope, dreamers, apostles, and entrepreneurs (women who will birth new things).

As I reviewed the list of what this mighty army of women would look like, I prayed about what it meant for me. As I began to speak publicly at various places, I would share the prayer retreat story and pray over the women. God continues to raise up the mighty army of women full of the Spirit. God draws us to open our hearts, eyes, and ears to the talented and gifted women around us—in families, churches, and communities.

You are a part of that mighty army as well. God has created you as an individual to do something I could never do, to go somewhere I cannot go.

Why am I telling you this story? You are a part of that mighty army as well. God has created you as an individual to do something I could never do, to go somewhere I cannot go. He has equipped and empowered your purpose and design; thus, "your deepest longing should be to be alive with God, to become the person God made you to be, and to be used to help God's world flourish."[12]

This type of flourishing does not happen without asking God for your mountain. When we ask for the Spirit of God to use us, we invite risk, pain, and the unfamiliar to change us. Growth happens when He nudges us to move away from the comfortable places and step out into the unknown or begin the ascent up the mountain.

When Moses sent the twelve spies out to survey the land, Joshua and Caleb were the only two who came back full of faith, saying, "We can do this!" The other ten were ready to go back to Egypt and become slaves again. After the venture to spy the land, Caleb lived a long and full life. He climbed many mountains in his old age, and "as his generation all died out he had to develop a whole new circle of friends as an older man. He became mentor, guide, and cheerleader for an entirely

---

12 John Ortberg, *The Me I Want to Be: Becoming God's Best Version of You* (Grand Rapids, MI: Zondervan, 2010), 254.

new generation, and he did it to such an extent that they all said they wanted eighty-five-year-old Caleb to lead them when they went to the hill country."[13]

While we venture into a new place, a start, a fresh beginning, God waits for you at your mountain; however, "your mountain will not look exactly like anyone else's. But often you will recognize it because it lies at the intersection of the tasks that tap into your greatest strengths and the needs that tap into your deepest passions."[14] We go to our mountains together, not alone, but with a community of sisters cheering for one another.

To begin the individual and collective journey, I ask you to consider taking a journey on a twelve-hour prayer retreat to listen and rest. I have shared with you the outcome of one of my listening retreats (Psalm 68:11), so expect God to speak to you.

Personal prayer retreating was not a discipline in my life until several years ago when I started on a one-year leadership investment intensive with Alicia Britt Chole. The mentoring group met at Rivendell in Branson, Missouri, January 2015, for a three-day prayer retreat intensive. The first day proved disastrous because my task-oriented mind would wander back and forth from God and my to-do list. The next day, admitting defeat to the group, I decided to start again. The end resulted in a wonderful time invested in nearness with Jesus. Since then, I have practiced prayer retreating regularly in my life and leadership journey.

Alicia Britt Chole states in her book *Ready Set Rest, The Practice of Prayer Retreating*:

> When I first started the discipline of prayer-retreating, I thought of it as a luxury. Now, this Jesus-inspired habit of intentionally investing in extended time of prayer is a guarded given in my journey. Imagine, oh, imagine, how the future could be impacted by a generation of leaders whose public presence was anchored in spiritual rest.[15]

Sabbath and rest are another aspect of prayer retreating. I define sabbath rest as "life-giving." Sometimes during my sabbath and prayer retreats, I most need rest. At that time, the most spiritual thing I can do is take a nap.

Sabbath days for me often turn into a creative activity of restoring a piece of furniture or decorating a new area of my home. Other times I take a bike ride, hike,

---

13 Ortberg, *The Me I Want to Be*, 250.

14 Ortberg, *The Me I Want to Be*, 252.

15 Alicia Britt Chole, *Ready Set Rest, The Practice of Prayer Retreating* (Rogersville, MO: Onewholeworld, 2014), 44.

or walk along the beach. The key is to allow time for prayer, listening, and Bible reading, and to do something that will bring additional life to your soul.

The Collective Journey Up the Mountain

When I reflect about my ministry years from Bible college to the present, I think of the things required of busy leadership life and rearing a family. The words *soul care*, *spiritual retreats*, and *renewal* had been foreign to my vocabulary. It took twenty-eight years and a transition from local church ministry to district leadership before I realized the unhealthy state of my soul and the driving ministry motives. Arriving in this new season placed the ministry expectations on my husband, leaving little for me and allowing the state of my soul to stare me in the face.

Two years into the new leadership transition, a cancer diagnosis, the loss of my brother—I was floundering. I decided to invest in a one-year mentoring cohort with Alicia Chole and to go back to school and get a master's degree. These two avenues of new direction and study opened me up to the idea of prayer retreats and sabbath rest. During one of the prayer retreats, I took along the advent book, *The Greatest Gift*, by Ann Voskamp, which provided me some fresh perspective on what actually matters:

> *The mattering part is never what isn't. The mattering part is never the chopped off stump. It isn't what dream has been cut down, what hope has been cut off, what part of the heart has been cut out. The tender mattering part is—You have a tree.*[16]

God reminded me that I could elaborate on the cut-down tree, the pain, and its root, or I could recognize that I have a tree. Challenged to reflect on past and present ministry as a tree, I have many different trees represented in my journey. I noticed barren trees, new blossoming trees, trees full of fruit, and trees of changing colors. The cycle of seasons continues over many aspects of ministry. Each tree remains full of purpose, regardless if it is barren or blossoming with much fruit. In stillness and quiet tears, I allowed this peace to encompass my spirit.

---

16 Ann Voskamp, *The Greatest Gift, Unwrapping the Full Love Story of Christmas* (Carol Stream, IL: Tyndale, 2013), 4.

God reminded me that I could elaborate
on the cut down tree, the pain, and its root,
or I could recognize that I have a tree.

Through this new season, my tree didn't feel sturdy or full. The season was barren, and I had to give up much, causing the tree to lose its leaves. There my ministry tree stood barren in winter, walking me through depression, cancer, and grief. This barren tree stayed for three years, allowing me to die to self, my high expectations, my drive to perform, and task-orientation.

In spiritual journeys, however, winter does not last forever. Spring arrives, and with its arrival, new blossoms emerge. This represents my current ministry journey. A new season has come, and everything on which I embark provides a new place for planting.

Psalms 1 and 139 powerfully illustrate the point: "You hem me in—behind and before; you have laid your hand upon me. Such knowledge is too wonderful for me, too lofty for me to attain" (139:5, 6). Psalm 1:3 says, "He is like a tree planted by streams of water, which yields its fruit in season and whose leaf does not wither. Whatever he does prospers." The two scripture references speak of a balance between productivity, soul care, and self-care. Prayer, resting, and relaxation remain vital to the life of the leader, along with careful attention to the body, soul, and mind.

This truth is illustrated even in the life of Jesus, as recorded in Luke 5:15-16: "Yet the news about him spread all the more, so that crowds of people came to hear him and to be healed of their sicknesses, but Jesus often withdrew to lonely places and prayed."

The opposite of brokenness, of course, is wholeness. Peter Scazzero poignantly observes the impact personal wholeness has on leadership:

> When we devote ourselves to reaching the world for Christ while ignoring our
> own emotional and spiritual health, our leadership is shortsighted at best.
> At worst, we are negligent, needlessly hurting others and undermining God's
> desire to expand His kingdom through us.[17]

17 Peter Scazzero, "The Emotionally Healthy Leader," *Influence Magazine,* December 2015-January 2016, 41, 42.

For this reason, creating healthy connectivity with God, ourselves, and others remains imperative.

In his book *A Hidden Wholeness: The Journey Toward an Undivided Life*, Parker Palmer uses a blizzard analogy to explain the chaos of life and the connection with the survival of our soul. He says that in a blizzard, the farmers would tie a rope from the back door of the house to the door on the barn, so they would not get lost and freeze to death during a whiteout.

It is this way with the chaos of life and the care of our soul. We need to tie a rope between our soul and God, between our soul and others, so we can survive the blizzard:

> *When we catch sight of the soul, we can become healers in the wounded world—in the family, in the neighborhood, in the workplace, and in political life—as we are called back to our "hidden wholeness" amid the violence of the storm.*[18]

At the end of Moses' life, during one of his last leadership hurrahs, we see him on the highest peak at Mount Nebo, where God led him to survey the Promised Land one final time. Scripture says he was 120 years old, but his vigor was unimpaired (Deuteronomy 34:7). He could still climb mountains.

Why would I talk about the end when we are at the beginning of our collective journey? We often think finishing well has everything to do with endings. But finishing well as leaders has everything to do with our ability to spiritually climb mountains: "Life is not about comfort. It is about saying, 'God give me another mountain.'"[19]

Let's live the adventure that God has planned for us and flourish in life and leadership.

Let's live the adventure that God has planned for us and flourish in life and leadership. You're not alone on your mountain journey. It's a collective journey, and we will go together as a band of explorers ready for what God has for each of us. The best part, though, is that God waits for you at your mountain. He will not leave you alone in the journey but walks beside you the entire way.

---

18 Parker J. Palmer, *A Hidden Wholeness: The Journey Toward an Undivided Life* (San Francisco: Jossey-Bass, 2004), 43.

19 Ortberg, *The Me I Want to Be*, 252.

PART ONE

CORE-SELF: THE POWER OF INWARD REFLECTION

Watch over your heart with all diligence, for from it flow the springs of life.
—Proverbs 4:23 (NASB)

Welcome to the first foundation in *The Collective Journey*—Core-Self, The Power of Inward Reflection. I suggest you take the journey through this book slowly. It is not something to rush through, but each foundation and added exercises or questions are thought out to bring about the desired results. Use the book individually or with a group.

The first two foundations will help define and assess the inner you. The journey from core-self will move toward communion—the power of story. Both aspects of the two foundations support spiritual formation—"the process by which your inner self and character are shaped."[20]

You have an inner you and an outer you. The outer you is influenced by eating, drinking, exercise, sleep, and how you live. The inner you (spirit) concerns your character, will, thoughts, and desires. It is formed by what you see, read, think, hear, and do. You design your inner life regardless of whether you nourish it or neglect it.

---

20 Ortberg, *The Me I Want to Be*, 29.

Here's what I know: God made you to flourish.

Here's what I know: God made you to flourish, "to receive life from outside yourself, creating vitality within yourself and producing blessing beyond yourself. Flourishing is God's gift and plan, and when you flourish you are in harmony with God, other people, creation, and yourself."[21] God will not change who you are. He will, however, make you a better version of yourself.

During the core-self foundation, you will take at least two personality tests to help you understand who you are and reflect on the many influences that form your unique self. The goal centers on answering the question of every Christ-follower: "Who am I?" and illustrates that who we are matters much more than what we do.[22]

You will also spend time reflecting on the condition of your soul and answer the question: "How is it with my soul?" You will discover that you can only reach your God-given potential by becoming aware of your soul and caring for the inner self (spirit). Through guided activities, you will see that the soul is where the true self resides.

Leaning in with truthfulness—allowing the questions and stirrings of the soul to guide—brings forth honest and congruent growth. Developing this process will help sustain wholeness in life and leadership.

You will explore what is life-giving, the grace of God, love of God, and peace of God. Chapter five constitutes one of the most important chapters in *The Collective Journey*. The difficulties of leadership and life need a heaven-down understanding of grace and the power it gives to receive the love and peace of God.

> The difficulties of leadership and life need a heaven-down understanding of grace and the power it gives to receive the love and peace of God.

---

21 Ortberg, *The Me I Want to Be*, 14.

22 Reese and Loane, *Deep Mentoring*, 49.

At the end of *The Collective Journey*, you will develop a vision and values statement for your personal and leadership journey. I'll explain more about how you will define this later in the book, but begin to think about and pay attention to the various discoveries made about yourself in each foundation, and write them in a journal or in the note sections of your phone.

Leadership and you are not two different entities. You are your leadership—the inner you and the outer you. What you bring to the world is uniquely you. The journey to become the best version of me is continual and constant, so will the journey be for you, my friend.

As you begin this first foundation, I have included some extra suggestions to enhance the foundation. These are called, *Living It Out Rhythms.* The rhythms, *Soulful You, Mindful You, Heartful You,* and *Creative You,* are designed for different individuals and how we best understand the material we study. If you are contemplative at your core, then the *Soulful You* rhythms may be best for you to explore a deeper understanding of the core-self foundation. *Mindful You* celebrates the thinker and researcher—the part that desires to see the evidence on paper. *Heartful You* is designed to speak to the heart of what matters, and *Creative You* is for the artsy ones in the group.

Although you can pick and choose which ones you want to do, I suggest that everyone in foundation one, core-self, not skip the prayer retreat and the personality testing.

I have also included one suggested book for you to read as you go deeper into the study of core-self and the importance of inward reflection of the soul.

Core-Self Assessment

- A better understanding of the inner you (spirit) and how it relates to your relationship with God, yourself, and others.
- Deeper awareness of the inner you (spirit) and when things are out of alignment with God.
- Incorporating one's self-discipline toward better self-care, e.g., weekly sabbaths, exercise or healthier eating plan, giving oneself routine time for life-giving refreshment.

Living It Out Rhythms–Core-Self

Table 1. Foundation One: Core-Self

CORE-SELF	CORE-SELF	CORE-SELF	CORE-SELF
Soulful You	Mindful You	Heartful You	Creative You
Begin the journey of creating sabbath/rest into your routine. How will this look for you? Take a spiritual prayer retreat. If you can schedule a 24-hour retreat—wonderful! If not, grab at least an 8-hour uninterrupted time frame. Use a journal and pen, your laptop, or phone to record important thoughts about this space. Remember to write down what the Spirit reveals about you—your inner and outer self. Take the Life-Giving Assessment (Appendix A) and then pick one and do something life-giving. Take the day and enjoy the freedom from work and leadership life. The ideas are endless!	Take two of the online personality tests. The tests are free, so follow the links provided. www.personalitypathways.com www.16personalities.com/freepersonality-test www.humanmetrics.com/cgi-win/jtypes2.asp www.onlinepersonalitytests.org/disc www.enneagraminstitute.com www.truity.com/test/enneagram-personality-test Review the results with someone close to you to see if the results are accurate to your true self. We will also discuss this in our group and one-on-one mentoring sessions. Take some reflective time to consider a healthier you. What are some steps to take to create a plan? Some possibilities are a 20- to 30-minute walk, eliminate sugar from your diet (this one is hard for me), or take a break from social media. These are a few examples.	Take some time to reflect and answer the questions from the Spiritual Discipline of Self-Care[23] Resource (Appendix B). At your leisure, pick one, two, or three of the exercises to complete. Each day, take one of the scriptures from the *I Am* Scripture Resource and pray the scripture over yourself. (Appendix C)	Choose a scripture or word that has been significant to you during this core-self journey. Go to a craft store and purchase a canvas, along with paints or pencils, and create a picture with the word, scripture, or visual that reflects this foundation. Place the picture somewhere you can see it daily as a reminder of what God is doing in you.

---

23 Adele Ahlberg Calhoun, *Spiritual Disciplines Handbook: Practices That Transform Us* (Downers Grove, IL: InterVarsity Press, 2005), 72, 73.

Core-Self Book Suggestion

Barton, Ruth Haley. *Strengthening the Soul of Your Leadership: Seeking God in the Crucible of Ministry.* Downers Grove, IL: InterVarsity Press, 2008.

CHAPTER 3

HOW IS IT WITH YOUR SOUL?

"For what does it profit a man if he gains the whole world
[wealth, fame, success], and loses or forfeits himself?"
—Luke 9:25 (AMP)

The leadership mentoring journey must start with understanding the importance of being a keeper of one's soul. As little children, we are often taught the prayer, "Now I lay me down to sleep. I pray the Lord my soul to keep." The prayer goes on to teach that our soul will continue to heaven or hell after our death. Although this is true, our soul has much greater purpose.

The early Wesleyans would get together for small group prayer meetings. At the start of every gathering, they asked an important question: "How is it with your soul?" We have the tradition of asking, "How are you?" But that question can be easily disregarded with an indifferent response.

As leaders, we often avoid the people who will give us a lengthy response to the "How are you today?" question. However, the query, "How is it with your soul?" prods us to examine our soul actively and truthfully. One cannot easily sidestep the question or response.

In leadership, all of us hope our souls are in good standing and at a healthy place, but the reality is, even if we are keeping pace fairly well, we have watched others around us throw it all away because of the immense pressure. We have seen friends break under the overwhelming load of family pressures, ministry heartbreak, mixed-up priorities, and the push of all work and no rest:

What would it look like for me to lead more consistently from my soul—the place of my own encounter with God—rather than leading primarily from my head, my unbridled activism, or my performance-oriented drivenness? What would it be like to find God in the context of my leadership rather than miss God in the context of my leadership? The soulful leader pays attention to such inner realities and the questions that they raise rather than ignoring them and continuing the charade or judging himself or herself harshly. . . . Spiritual leadership emerges from our willingness to stay involved with our own soul—that place where God's Spirit is at work stirring up our deepest questions and longings to draw us deeper into relationship with him.[24]

Soul living requires active awareness–
real-time honesty and paying
attention to inner realities instead
of ignoring what truly goes on.

Soul living requires active awareness—real-time honesty and paying attention to inner realities instead of ignoring what truly goes on. Farming, like soul care, takes much time and effort. As author Stephen Covey says,

Could you ever "cram" on the farm—forget to plant in the spring, play all summer, and then race in the fall to bring in the harvest? No, because the farm is a natural system. You must pay the price and follow the process. You reap what you sow, there is no short cut.[25]

---

24 Ruth Haley Barton, *Strengthening the Soul of Your Leadership: Seeking God in the Crucible of Ministry* (Downers Grove, IL: InterVarsity Press, 2008), 25.

25 Stephen Covey, "The Law of the Farm," *Upprevention*, https://upprevention.org/the/34154-the-law-of-the-farm-by-stephen-covey-714-141.php.

No matter what I choose to do, the day will come when the soil will produce a crop, and if my work is completed well, the reaped fruit will be godly fruit.

How do we get in the flow, then? How do we assess how our inner (spirit) life handles the stress of life and leadership? How do we know when we need to take a break and fill our spiritual tanks once again? We can't simply assess the health of our soul by Bible reading and prayer time because even the Pharisees were strong in these disciplines.

John Ortberg asked a wise man for his response to soul assessment. The man responded that he asked himself these two questions: "Am I growing more easily discouraged these days? Am I growing more easily irritated these days?"[26]

I invite you to begin to incorporate these two questions into your assessment of how it is with your soul. When the answer is *yes* to either of those questions, reflect on what spiritual disciplines have been ignored: *What life-giving practices are missing from my life? Do I need to reprioritize my priorities? Maybe I simply need a good long nap!*

Only you can give truthful answers. I caution you to listen closely when answering. Do not dodge, duck, or evade the question, for it remains the most important question you will ever ask in your life and leadership journey.

Reflection Questions:

1) Am I growing more easily discouraged these days?
2) Am I growing more easily irritated these days?
3) How is it with my soul?

---

26 Ortberg, *The Me I Want to Be*, 21.

CHAPTER 4
WHO AM I?

We pray for you all the time—pray that our God will make you fit for
what he's called you to be, pray that he'll fill your good ideas and acts of
faith with his own energy so that it all amounts to something.
—2 Thessalonians 1:11 (MSG)

I remember the day I took my first personality test. I came downstairs to the kitchen and exclaimed, "I'm an extrovert!" My daughter, Lindsay, turned around, looked at me, and said, "And you're surprised by this revelation?"

The Myers-Briggs personality test had revealed not only my extraversion tendency but the idea that I possibly have several versions of myself as an ESTJ, ESFJ, ENFJ, or ENTJ. The professor said that only I will truly know when and how my "shadow" operates and why. Typically, the two middle letters reveal the shadow, especially when not scoring high on the four options.

For further study, the spirituality assessment in the book, *Knowing Me, Knowing God*, confirmed the shadow of my personality. It revealed a strong tendency toward extraversion and judging preferences in how I prefer to worship and engage spiritually. The slight shadow scores remain in the middle preferences of Sensing/Intuition and Feeling/Thinking. As Malcolm Goldsmith notes, we must engage our shadow to become healthy leaders:

We too can find health and healing, strength and courage if we begin to work with, and on, our unconscious, on what many people call "our shadow." In order to get the best view of a stained-glass window, it is necessary to walk into the darkness of a church and look out toward the light. So too it is often necessary for us to explore the inner darknesses of our personality, and this can allow the light to illuminate them. In this way we can have a better understanding of ourselves and develop a spirituality that is honest and attempts to offer to God the totality of our being. This includes not only those parts that we are pleased with and find acceptable but also those bits of ourselves which we have previously relegated into our subconscious.[27]

Knowing one's true self—drawing from strengths and viewing our weaknesses with honesty—allows the leader to grow in unexpected areas. The comfort of operating in my shadow has yielded much growth in my leadership, adding a grace-giving function that wouldn't normally be present.

> Knowing one's true self–drawing from strengths and viewing our weaknesses with honesty–allows the leader to grow in unexpected areas.

After giving ample examples of the life of Jesus and the way He functioned in various areas, Goldsmith uncovers the end goal in this evaluation of self and leadership:

We, too, operate in all the functions, but because we prefer some to the others we often find it difficult to act appropriately in any given situation. We have a tendency to want to meet every person and every situation using our preferred functions, but sometimes it is more appropriate to use the other ones. Jesus seemed to know how to respond appropriately in whatever situation he found himself, and in that way, he is a role model and an example for us all to follow.[28]

In my leadership journey, the abilities I offer remain effective but prove *most* effective when flowing from Jesus' model of authenticity and grace. I get up every day

---

27 Malcolm Goldsmith, *Knowing Me, Knowing God: Exploring Your Spirituality with Myers-Briggs* (Nashville: Abingdon Press, 1997), 86.

28 Goldsmith, *Knowing Me, Knowing God*, 104.

and put on my leadership clothes filled with holes and covered with dirt, showing others that, for part of this journey, I've been living in a cave. Cave living happens when the struggles of life seem to drain all the light out of our daily existence.

I cannot dismiss my battles with depression, cancer diagnoses, grief and loss, and leadership wounds. The generation coming behind me isn't interested in my accomplishments; they want to know the truth through authentic leadership and a grace-filled message. Often this will mean sharing the not-so-pretty cave dwellings and shadows yet letting others know that Jesus waits on the other side.

As you continue on the core-self journey, a self-evaluation and self-development plan must be gauged by living authentically in *shalom*, sabbath, and grace:

> In order to build a life characterized by sacred rhythms, we need to understand three foundational principles—Shalom, Sabbath, and Grace. Shalom is an inner experience of well-being that overflows in our outer world. . . . Sabbath is the baseline beat in God's rhythm of rest. . . . Grace is the experience of being yoked to Christ. . . our daily work is no longer at odds with wholeness and rest.[29]

The authentic, grace-filled life richly overflows with messiness and cave dwelling but remains filled with practicing the presence of God, regardless of the pain-filled or joy-filled journey. The presence of God is a place of freedom, faith, and anticipation of what lies ahead.

Paul writes, "We pray for you all the time—pray that our God will make you fit for what he's called you to be, pray that he'll fill your good ideas and acts of faith with his own energy so that it all amounts to something" (2 Thessalonians 1:11, MSG).

Leaders who lead from this humble posture ultimately discover their definitions of true self do not replicate the latest leadership success story. Authentic, grace-filled leaders get up every day and dress in leadership clothes that properly fit, and they wear them with grace and style.

Reflection Questions:

1) What would you define as a place of cave dwellings for you?

2) How have these places made you better in your life and leadership?

3) If not better, how can you form a plan to allow for God to bring healing to these areas that He desires to use for His glory in your life?

---

29 Kerri Weems, *Rhythms of Grace* (Grand Rapids, MI: Zondervan, 2014), 29.

CHAPTER 5
WHAT IS LIFE-GIVING?

But by the [remarkable] grace of God I am what I am, and
His grace toward me was not without effect.
—1 Corinthians 15:10 (AMP)

The last chapter of the core-self foundation asks the question: "What is life-giving?" The answer is not an activity but a disposition when we take on the nature of God. Yes, God loves me. Yes, God grants me peace. But the grace of God, when applied, gives way to every aspect of life and leadership. We receive God's grace, apply it to ourselves, and then learn to give it away to others.

The *what* in being led by me is no longer gauging success by human accolades. Instead, I long for the next prayer retreat when I can hear God's whispers over my life. I know where I fall short and how I am insignificant, but through grace, God reveals what matters most. Through this grace model, I can begin to operate in what God designed me to do. What flows in also flows out, giving space for a new perspective, one that is heaven-downward (God's perspective) rather than earth-up (my and others' perspectives).

Grace has a simple definition—unmerited favor, privilege, favor undeserved. Maybe you feel a little like me. I have always needed a double dose of grace. Like

Paul, I am able to say, "But by the [remarkable] grace of God I am what I am, and His grace toward me was not without effect" (1 Corinthians 15:10, AMP).

> Maybe you feel a little like me. I have always needed a double dose of grace.

Thomas Brooks, a Puritan preacher, beautifully illustrates the idea of powerful grace, saying, "Grace and glory differ very little, one is the seed, the other the flower. Grace is glory militant. Glory is grace triumphant." Good, right? Grace is the seed and glory is the flower.

Because of how we allow grace to grow in our lives (receive it, apply it, nourish it), grace makes us a better version of ourselves—we get to do what we do. Grace is not a little whiny weakling. One dose of grace remains powerful and life-giving. Grace shows up and makes what we get to do militant—active, radical, revolutionary. The glory that shines over us from grace is triumphant—successful, winning, victorious, conquering.

If you are not experiencing the love and peace of God, then you need more grace. Grace moves into our lives and radically changes us from what we used to be to what we are now becoming—a better version of ourselves. The seed of grace is planted in the inner you (spirit), and the glory that comes from grace shines all over the outer you. This makes me want to go out on my porch and shout—"GRACE, GRACE, GRACE! It's life-giving!"

> Grace moves into our lives and radically changes us from what we used to be to what we are now becoming–a better version of ourselves.

I remember giving some grace to my son, Andrew. He did not deserve it, and he knew it, but I felt the Holy Spirit nudge me to show him grace. I remember his reaction when I applied grace to him. He instinctively threw his arms up over his head in a Rocky Balboa motion (I'm sure I heard the theme music playing) and shouted, "Yes!" in a triumphant and victorious motion. With grace, my friend, you will win—every time.

In the previous chapter, I asked you to think about your cave-dwelling places (the not-so-good times of life and leadership). Take a moment now, and allow the Holy Spirit to apply grace to the wounds, hurts, unforgiveness, and—possibly—shame you feel when you reflect on these hard places.

Isaiah 55:12-13 says:

> *You will go out in joy and be led forth in peace; the mountains and hills will burst into song before you, and all the trees of the field will clap their hands. Instead of the thornbush will grow the juniper, **and instead of briers the myrtle will grow**. This will be for the Lord's renown, for an everlasting sign, that will endure forever. (Emphasis mine.)*

To conclude this foundation, let us concentrate on this truth: *instead of briers the myrtle will grow*. The roots of the myrtle tree run deeply, entrenched in a firm foundation, so that nothing sways or moves it. When the water on the surface has dried up, the myrtle tree is rooted and will draw water from deep within to sustain it.

The core-self foundation is not a step to skip in *The Collective Journey*. The surface water will often dry up, leaving behind only what remains below—the deep places no one will ever see. In those times, you will need to be well-watered by God to sustain the drought.

Reflection Questions:

1) How is grace winning (victorious) in your life?
2) What particular spiritual discipline have you started this month that has become life-giving for you in life and leadership?
3) What is your plan to continue implementing this life-giving practice into your life and leadership?

PART TWO

COMMUNION: THE POWER OF YOUR STORY

The angel of the Lord found Hagar near a spring in the desert; it was the spring that is beside the road to Shur. And he said, "Hagar, slave of Sarai, where have you come from, and where are you going?"
—Genesis 16:7-8

Communion is the second part of the inner movement. The practice of the communion sacrament brings a powerful analogy to how we can embrace the power of our story as seen through God's story—His death, burial, and resurrection. Together we will consider the practices of remembering, forgiveness, and gratitude.

As we begin this foundational chapter, consider the question: "How is it with your story?" To understand and answer this question, all four of the *Living It Out Rhythms* will be wrapped around one activity—creating a personal story map.

As you read the instructions carefully and begin working on the project, allow the Holy Spirit to go with you as you reflect on your life journey, family of origin, culture, successes, failures, faith experience, sources of joy and pain, and emotional and spiritual growth.

When I completed my personal story map, I found difficult places and wounds that needed God's grace, but I also found many gratitude moments as I reflected on the goodness of God.

As you create your personal story map, the story of Hagar in Genesis will illustrate the meaning of the two questions: Where did you come from? Where are you going? (16:8). Hagar knew from where she had come—"I'm running away from my mistress Sarai" (v. 8)—but God showed her where she was going (vv. 9-12).

Leading with an open heart requires careful reflection on knowing where you came from, knowing where you stand, and knowing where you want to go as you take others with you.

Leading with an open heart requires careful reflection on knowing where you came from, knowing where you stand, and knowing where you want to go as you take others with you. As leaders, awareness of how our personal and family culture shaped us remains paramount for leading from a healthy and whole heart. As you are willing to work through these questions with an open heart, God will use you to transform the culture where you lead.

I love the book *A Work of Heart: Understanding How God Shapes Spiritual Leaders* by Reggie McNeal. He writes:

> *Fortunately, many women and men provide real spiritual leadership. These leaders are masterpieces in too short a supply. They are genuine works of heart. They don't develop overnight, though it might seem they appear "out of nowhere." They always come from somewhere—the heart of God. They are carefully crafted, faithfully shaped.*[30]

The chapter "Culture: Meeting the World" in that same book provides an excellent reminder on how followers replicate the culture of the leader, which is why it remains important to reflect on our story and lead from the heart of God.

The communion emblems represent forgiveness, healing, and health. Partaking of the bread reminds participants that, because His body was broken, believers can live in health and healing. The cup represents His shed blood and serves as reminder that we live in forgiveness. As you continue in the communion (the power of your

---

30 Reggie McNeal, *A Work of Heart: Understanding How God Shapes Spiritual Leaders* (San Francisco: Jossey-Bass, 2000, 2011), xii.

story) foundation, be encouraged to "reimagine holiness not through the lens of perfectionism but through the lens of our utter oneness with God."[31]

The table of the Lord offers a way to come back to that place and remember, examine, and ensure that one's story is good. Remembering and forgiving enable participants to pray generously and celebrate in gratitude.

Communion Assessment

- Use memories from birth until present to complete the exercise of a personal story map. Allow the Holy Spirit to bring revelation to specific memories, revealing both unhealthy wounds and ones that bring gratitude.
- Walk through healing and forgiveness from the memories revealed in the personal story map.
- Start a gratitude journal.

Living It Out Rhythms–Communion

Table 2. Foundation Two: Communion (In this foundation, all four rhythms have the same assignment.)

COMMUNION	COMMUNION	COMMUNION	COMMUNION
Soulful You	Mindful You	Heartful You	Creative You
PERSONAL STORY MAP: Create a personal story map of your life from birth to present. You can use a timeline format on paper or another creative way. It is important to include main events, but also allow the Holy Spirit to help you remember things that may seem insignificant. This project is for your eyes only. We can discuss in the one-on-one mentoring session together, if you like, but that is up to you.	PERSONAL STORY MAP: I suggest you take a Spiritual Prayer Retreat (4 to 8 hours) to compile the personal story map. If this is not possible, at least set aside 2-hour time intervals to give attention to this. Also, consider your family of origin. What kind of people raised you? Were they educated, working-class, or did they struggle with finances? Ethnicity, city or country, siblings, parents divorced, grandparents, friends? Schools, did you move around a lot? Don't forget to include your spiritual journey. Salvation experience, calling, other significant memories.	PERSONAL STORY MAP: Pay close attention to the joy and pain revealed while compiling your story map. Release shame, unforgiveness, hurts, and allow the Holy Spirit to heal your story. How did this affect you? Journal and pray over your discoveries, pausing for areas in need of healing. Pay particular attention to memories that bring you joy or pain.	PERSONAL STORY MAP: As you pray about forgiveness or enjoy a time of gratitude, find a picture of you or family that has a particular memory attached and thank God for all that He has brought you through. Start a gratitude journal.

Communion Book Suggestion

McNeal, Reggie. *A Work of Heart: Understanding How God Shapes Spiritual Leaders.*
San Francisco: Jossey-Bass, 2011.

CHAPTER 6

HOW IS IT WITH YOUR STORY?

Your eyes saw my unformed body; all the days ordained for me
were written in your book before one of them came to be.
—Psalm 139:16

The last chapter of the core-self foundation introduced Isaiah 55:12-13 with careful attention to verse 13: "Instead of the thornbush will grow the juniper, *and instead of briers the myrtle will grow.* This will be for the Lord's renown, for an everlasting sign, that will endure forever."

The myrtle tree has countless grain patterns. Each tree's pattern develops by the events that occur in its surroundings. That means each storm, each drought, adverse or good conditions, contribute to the beautiful designs in the wood of the myrtle tree.

Sometimes the tree is then fashioned in the hands of a craftsman—cutting, sanding, shaping—until the myrtle wood becomes a beautiful creation. Often these crafted pieces of wood or furniture become treasured heirlooms because of the years it took to get the wood to maturity before being processed by the craftsman.[32]

---

32 Lynn Nessa, "A Lesson from the Myrtle Tree," *Inspirational Contemplation*, https://nessalynn77.wordpress.com/2011/02/12/a-lesson-from-the-myrtle-tree/.

> When I was younger, I thought that one day
> I would finally "arrive" on my Christ-like
> journey, but I was wrong. We will not be
> like Jesus until we see Him face to face.

Likewise, our life remains a continual process to maturity. When I was younger, I thought that one day I would finally "arrive" on my Christ-like journey, but I was wrong. We will not be like Jesus until we see Him face to face, so we continue to strive for maturity, allowing the trials and the good we experience to contribute to our raw beauty.

Take some time to meditate on Psalm 139:16: "Your eyes saw my unformed body; all the days ordained for me were written in your book before one of them came to be." Wow! God is with you, sees you, knows all about you, and walks with you in past, present, and future.

In the *Living It Out Rhythms*, I have commissioned you to complete a personal story map during this foundation of communion. To incorporate the communion analogy here, we see three aspects of partaking—remembering, forgiveness, and gratitude.

Remembering is at the heart of the sacrament of communion:

> *When he had given thanks, he broke it and said, "This is my body, which is for you; do this in remembrance of me." In the same way, after supper he took the cup, saying, "This cup is the new covenant in my blood; do this, whenever you drink it, in remembrance of me." —Luke 22:19-20*

Recalling is crucial to heart-shaping. Examining, forgiving, and having gratitude happen at the Lord's table. Because of His ultimate sacrifice and the power of Jesus' story, we can relinquish our story to Him. Remembering may be difficult for some, and you may want to skip over various parts of your story, but remembering is important to your life and leadership:

> *Many Christian leaders do not understand their own developing life story. They do not have a clear picture of the heart-shaping subplots that in the long run create their life and leadership legacy. They sometimes see individual or significant events as important, but they often fail to connect the dots of their life experience. As a result, they miss the learnings that such understanding*

yields. . . . Self-understanding begins and ends with God. I am convinced that the most effective leaders are those who take time to ponder what God is up to in their own lives. Those who understand their own hearts will be better prepared to lead.[33]

Understanding your story is part of the process for understanding your leadership heart. Although parts may be painful, it is important to share your story and see its significance and power.

In the book *A Work of Heart*, Reggie McNeal notes that "maturity comes when we can learn to appreciate how our hearts were formed, to look at our early cultural development as a gift."[34]

Understanding your story is part of the process for understanding your leadership heart.

The three heart tasks for leaders include: knowing where you come from, knowing where you stand, and knowing where you want to go and take others with you.[35] Take some time this week to dig into your family of origin: Where did they come from? Were they working-class people, educated, or both? Are you a first-generation believer in Christ? If not, who was the first Christ-follower in your family? Think through other questions that the Holy Spirit brings to your memory, and allow your personal story map to help you appreciate how your heart was formed.

Reflection Questions:
1) Where did I come from?
2) Where am I going?
3) How was my heart formed?

---

33 Reggie McNeal, *A Work of Heart*, xxiii, xxv.

34 McNeal, *A Work of Heart*, 77.

35 McNeal, *A Work of Heart*, 75.

CHAPTER 7
A JOURNEY WITH GOD TO FIND FORGIVENESS

She gave this name to the Lord who spoke to her: "You are the God who sees me," for she said, "I have now seen the One who sees me." That is why the well was called Beer Lahai Roi; it is still there, between Kadesh and Bered.
—Genesis 16:13-14

I first heard about coracles in my spiritual formations class at the seminary where I received my master's degree. Dr. Carolyn Tennant, the professor, shared the history of the ancient Celtic church and the small boats constructed by the Welsh, Irish, and Scottish. The coracles were usually built for one or two people and could be carried from place to place:

> *The Celtic monks were by no means opposed to adventure, and they liked to build larger coracles that would hold more people and set out into the ocean. This would be adventurous by itself, but additionally the coracles were rudderless and often the monks would take no oars or paddles. They hoisted their sails and caught the winds and the currents, believing that God would take them where they were supposed to go to share the gospel.*[36]

---

36 Carolyn Tennant, *Catch the Wind of the Spirit: How the 5 Ministry Gifts Can Transform Your Church* (Springfield, MO: Vital Resources, 2016), 9.

Dr. Tennant revealed that they did this because the Irish took John 3:8 literally: "The wind blows wherever it pleases. You hear its sound, but you cannot tell where it comes from or where it is going." The travel or pilgrimage, called *peregrination*, was used to evangelize most of Europe and would "become one of the greatest and most effective mission movements of all time.

"However, the pilgrimage was also personal."[37]

The peregrination was "the outward symbol of an inner change, a metaphor and a symbol for the journey towards deeper faith and greater holiness and that journey toward God which is the Christian life."[38] According to Ian Bradley, the coracle pilgrimage was the act of "seeking the place of one's resurrection"—going on a journey with God to find God.[39] The wind blows in our story, too, in every aspect of it.

Journeys have always been a part of God's plan.

Journeys have always been a part of God's plan. Abraham and Sarah, Moses, the Israelites, and Joshua (from Egypt to the Promised Land), David (hiding in caves from Saul), Jesus (from birth in a stable to the cross), early church disciples, and Paul—these all took various journeys to further the gospel message, as well as to simply journey with God.

Part of the journey through communion and your personal story map includes forgiveness, an essential part. Unforgiveness is connected to shame. Undeserved shame often leads to resentment and to leaders who are unappealing to their followers.

We cannot undo the shame brought on by a circumstance or another person. When we have been wounded, we will carry the woundedness as a part of our reality. The only truth we can alter is the truth of our feelings. Changing our feelings can only come through forgiveness. As Lewis Smedes notes,

None of the options to forgiving does us any good. Revenge does not heal; it only makes things worse. Forgetting does not help. If we think we have forgotten, we have probably stuffed the memory beneath our consciousness to fester there as

37 Tennant, *Catch the Wind of the Spirit,* 11.

38 Ian Bradley, *The Celtic Way* (London: Darton, Longman and Todd, 1993), 80.

39 Bradley, *The Celtic Way,* 77.

the poisonous source of assorted other pains. Besides, some things should never be forgotten. The only option we have left is the creative act of forgiving our shamers with the same grace that enables us to forgive ourselves.[40]

Smedes gives five steps we go through when deciding to forgive.[41]

1) We blame the shamer: We hold him or her accountable. If we do not hold people accountable for what they did to us, we will not forgive them.

2) We surrender our right to get even: We take our natural right to a balanced account—a right to fairness, mind you, that is all, only what we deserve— we take it in our hands, look it over, consider its possibilities, and then we surrender it. We agree to live with the score untied.

3) We revise our caricature of the person who shamed us: We turn them into a monster personified by what they did to us. We see them; we feel them; we define their whole person in terms of how they shamed us. However, as we move with the forgiving flow, we gradually change our monsters back into the weak and faulty human beings they are (or were), not all that different from ourselves.

4) We revise our feelings. As the frozen tundra of resentment melts, a tendril of compassion breaks through the crust. Sorrow blends with anger. Sympathy softens resentment. We begin to feel in our consciousness a hesitant desire for the other person's welfare.

5) We accept the person who made us feel unacceptable. In the last scene of the drama, we offer our shamer the grace God has offered us. We not only pardon them, but we also accept them. Chances are that we are not able to restore the special relationship we had before. But if we cannot be reconciled, it will not be our resentment that prevents it.

We are the keeper of our stream, and we have the responsibility to keep the stream free of the debris that pollutes the water and makes it undrinkable.

The story of Hagar (Genesis 16) is a story of shame and forgiveness. Hagar found herself pregnant and cast out of the only place she had known. At a well in the desert, an angel of the Lord visited her and asked two questions: "Hagar, slave of Sarai, where have you come from, and where are you going?" These two questions reflect the healing power of story.

---

40 Lewis B. Smedes, *Shame and Grace: Healing the Shame We Don't Deserve* (New York: Harper Collins Publishers, 1993), 135-136.

41 Smedes, *Shame and Grace*, 136-137.

In the ancient world, wells were a place of necessity, social gathering, revelation, and connection. Every aspect of daily living involved the well. Women were the principal water carriers, going back and forth to the well many times a day. Is it possible Hagar had been there often and talked with her friends (other water carriers) and went to the well hoping to find someone with whom she could share her story? On that day, no one arrived except an angel of the Lord.

Genesis 16:14 describes the well as sitting between Kadesh, which means "sacred place in the desert," and Bered, meaning "to be cold." This well, where God allows Himself to be seen, sits between the sacred place in the desert and the cold place. In between these two places, God allows Himself to be seen in Hagar's story.

It is in our in-between places that we often birth "Ishmaels" as well. Your story may reveal several Ishmaels. Ishmael was not deemed the promised child; he was conceived by Hagar through the doubt and fear of Abraham and Sarah, but God redeems every aspect of our story, every Ishmael and Isaac.

Take some time to sit with the parts of your story in which the birthing of an Ishmael was conceived. Allow the Holy Spirit to bring forgiveness for yourself and others. Hagar named the place where God met her "Beer Lahai Roi," which means "the well of the Living One who sees me." Some Bible commentators believe that the translation of the name of the well is "the well of the Living one who *allows Himself to be seen." God allows Himself to be seen in your story*, my friend. You can count on it.

God allows Himself to be seen in your
story, my friend. You can count on it.

Reflection Questions:

1) How has God allowed Himself to be seen in your story?
2) Think about a time when you were in an in-between place. Did you birth an Ishmael?
3) If yes, how did God redeem that part of your story?

CHAPTER 8
GRATITUDE AND JOY PARTIES

So, you'll go out in joy, you'll be led into a whole and complete life. The mountains and the hills will lead the parade, bursting with song. All the trees of the forest will join the procession, exuberant with applause. No more thistles, but giant sequoias, no more thorn bushes, but stately pines— monuments to me, to God, living and lasting evidence of God.
—Isaiah 55:12-13 (MSG)

O ur last chapter of the communion foundation emphasizes the idea of gratitude and the power of your story. I love a good "thanks" party, where high fives happen, and cheers of celebration are loudly declared. Part of *The Collective Journey* is to walk through the hard stuff together. To party, however, we must reach the top of the steep mountain climb.

To conclude the inner foundation—core-self and communion—let's take a deeper look at the totality of Isaiah 55:12-13 (MSG):

So, you'll go out in joy, you'll be led into a whole and complete life. The mountains and the hills will lead the parade, bursting with song. All the trees of the forest will join the procession, exuberant with applause. No more thistles, but giant sequoias, no more thorn bushes, but stately pines—monuments to

me, to God, living and lasting evidence of God. When I read this passage, I
visualize a gratitude parade that will go down in history as one of the best ever.

Several years ago, I climbed an enormous spiritual and life mountain. I was sitting outside one day, feeling like I had finally reached the top of my climb, when I turned to read this scripture in Isaiah.

In a way that only God could orchestrate, the wind was blowing and the leaves on the trees were rippling a bit as if a storm were coming. The NIV says, "All the trees of the field clap their hands." How do trees clap their hands? It happens when the wind blows and the leaves rustle against each other.

I sat there, with tears of joy and gratitude streaming down my face, realizing that I was in a God-moment. Creation was clapping for me. Creation was having a parade and shouting, "You did it, girl! Way to go. You climbed that mountain!" I knew another thorn bush was sprouting with the new growth of a myrtle tree.

Your powerful story is for the Lord's renown.

Your powerful story is for the Lord's renown. Your powerful story is a living and lasting evidence of God. Creation recognizes it, and so should you.

Another tree mentioned in this passage is the juniper tree. The juniper tree (an evergreen) grows in the mountains of Lebanon and is an emblem of majestic stature that sometimes reaches sixty feet tall. This tree produces a fruit similar to a pine cone. The fruit grows to about four to five inches in length and then breaks open, scattering its contents on the ground. The fruit or "sweet meat" is served on all occasions of joy. Instead of a thorn bush will grow a giant tree that bears the fruit of joy.

The myrtle tree that grows instead of thistles symbolizes peace and victory. It represents all that is regenerative and restorative. The myrtle tree is known for victory because of its fragrance, presentation, preservation, and endurance. God says, "Instead of briers, your fragrance, presentation, preservation, and endurance will grow a victorious and a peaceful life."

Has it been a while since you have had a joyful gratitude party? How long since you have been thankful for the good parts of your story and the broken parts? Put on some music and celebrate the goodness of God. Maybe, just maybe, the wind will blow a bit today and the trees of the field will clap their hands for you as you climb to the top of the mountain.

As we move into the two outer foundations of calling and community, the deep truths you have learned in the inner foundations of core-self and communion will enhance your outer life. You cannot skip over the care of your soul and the power of story. They provide the flow of your life and leadership.

You cannot skip over the care of your soul and the power of story. They provide the flow of your life and leadership.

Reflection Questions:

1) What was the last spiritual mountain you climbed?
2) Reflect on your journey and notice where God was walking with you and cheering you on.
3) For what would it be appropriate for you to have a joy gratitude party?

PART THREE

CALLING: THE POWER OF GOD'S DESIGN IN YOU

*"Before I shaped you in the womb, I knew all about you. Before
you saw the light of day, I had holy plans for you: A prophet
to the nations—that's what I had in mind for you."*
—Jeremiah 1:5 (MSG)

The *Collective Journey* continues with Calling—The Power of God's Design in You. This foundation begins the outward focus of the leader and builds upon the revelation of the inner foundations—core-self and communion.

At this point, you have discovered that it's not so much what we do but who we are that matters in life and leadership. When the journey is collective (done by a group of people acting as a group) with its group discussions, one-on-one mentoring, and personal assessments, we travel from one place to another with an individualized growth plan.

Most of us probably have stacks of leadership books on our library shelves and try to attend the latest conferences where influential persons in their fields share the latest success stories. Although reading leadership materials and attending conferences such as these prove useful, relying on these methods often leads to generic leadership development instead of organic growth.

When our calling and leadership strive to reproduce someone else's pattern for triumph instead of looking deeper within to develop our own strengths, weaknesses, and unique qualities, we simply dress in oversized clothes and boots in a futile attempt to make a one-size-fits-all approach work for our own contexts.

As female leaders, the litmus test for calling occurs in understanding the power of femininity. Leaders are leaders but are expressed as male and female; they bring both sameness and differences to the table. Calling—the power of God's design in you—cannot negate the reality that you are a woman. We do not need more men at the table or women who act and think like men. What we need at the table are women called by God.

We do not need more men at the table or women who act and think like men. What we need at the table are women called by God.

After Eric Metaxas wrote the book *Seven Men and the Secrets of Their Greatness*, which received an unexpected number of positive responses, he realized how a great hunger for heroes exists in culture. People then started asking him if he would write a book on seven women who were great. He started to ask his friends, "If I do, whose stories should I tell?" The responses proved disappointing:

In doing so I encountered an assumption about women's greatness that wasn't surprising. Many people suggested women who were the first ones to do something that men had already done. Amelia Earhart, who was the first woman to fly solo across the Atlantic in 1932, was mentioned, as was Sally Ride, who was the first American woman in space. What struck me as wrong about these suggestions was that they presumed women should somehow be compared to men. But it seemed wrong to view women in that way. The great men in Seven Men and the Secrets to Their Greatness *were not measured against women, so why should the women in* Seven Women *be measured against men? When I consider the seven women I chose, I see that most of them were great for reasons that derive precisely from their being women, not in spite of it; and what made them great has nothing to do with their being measured against or competing with men. In other words,*

their accomplishments are not gender-neutral but are rooted in their singularity
as women. All of them existed and thrived as women.[42]

Psalm 68:11 says, "The Lord announces the word and the women who proclaim it are a mighty throng." In the ancient world of the Israelites, the men typically fought the battle, but the women sang the victory song. Thus, Miriam, at the crossing of the Red Sea, picked up her tambourine and sang in victory: "Sing to the Lord for he is highly exalted. Both horse and driver he has hurled into the sea" (Exodus 15:21).

Likewise, Judges 5 features the Song of Deborah: "Villagers in Israel would not fight; they held back until I, Deborah, arose, until I arose, a mother in Israel" (5:7). Barak refused to enter battle without Deborah who, as a woman, warrior, and a judge of Israel, engaged in her femaleness—and when the battle was won, she made a song declaration. Both these women did not shrink back from their calling or their femaleness.

The aim of life and leadership for the calling foundation is to wear properly fitted clothing, not oversized generic ones. The *what* in being led by me is no longer gauged by human accolades. Instead, I will allow my calling to flow out of the inside and be congruent with who I am. Through this model, I can begin to operate in what God designed me to do.

> I will allow my calling to flow out of the inside and be congruent with who I am.

What flows in also flows out, giving place to the vision and values statements that come from time spent with God and His design for me. I can then develop a plan that comes down from heaven (God's perspective) and not up from earth (my perspective).

For most of this foundation, you will develop a vision and values statement (Appendix H) for your life and leadership. I have included a sample of my vision and values statement as an example.

---

42 Eric Metaxas, *7 Women and the Secrets of Their Greatness* (Nashville: Thomas Nelson, 2015), xiv-xv.

To think through these two statements, begin with words that define you. What do people often say to describe you? What are you passionate about? What's your *one word*? If you're unclear on how to go about a vision and values statement and need more detailed instructions, feel free to research online. The goal is to understand the importance of being able to clearly communicate what we as leaders are designed to do.

Calling Assessment

- Create a vision and values statement.
- Dream with God—create a personal inventory with goals and action steps.

Living It Out Rhythms–Calling

Appendix D: The Vision and Values Statement

Table 3. Foundation Three: Calling

CALLING	CALLING	CALLING	CALLING
Soulful You	Mindful You	Heartful You	Creative You
Vision and Values Statement			
Take a spiritual prayer retreat. If you can schedule a 24-hour retreat—wonderful! If not, grab at least 4 to 8 hours of uninterrupted space to reflect and pray about your vision and values statement. Pray for a seasonal word from the Lord. Incorporate this word or phrase into your personal inventory.	Read the book, *Courage and Calling: Embracing Your God-Given Potential*. Gordon T. Smith. Continue working on your vision and values statement.	If possible, go back and visit a significant place of meaning in your life. Maybe it was where you accepted Christ or heard God whisper a specific dream into your heart. Capture it with a picture or write about your experience. Hey, I think it's even Instagram-worthy.	Did you discover your ONE word during this journey? If so, be creative as to how you display it so that it is a reminder to you about your vision and value statement and calling.

Calling Book Suggestions

Barsh, Joanna, and Susie Cranston. *How Remarkable Women Lead: The Breakthrough Model for Work and Life.* New York: Crown Business, 2009.

CHAPTER 9
MEANING AND PASSIONS

And the special gift of ministry you received when I laid hands
on you and prayed—keep that ablaze! God doesn't want us to
be shy with his gifts, but bold and loving and sensible.
—2 Timothy 1:6-7 (MSG)

You are a leader, or you would not be here. The question is whether we have clarity and passion about what, where, and how God desires us to lead. Leaders have a deep passion within that moves them to make a difference; how that passion is fueled and lived out in life and leadership is often done with no goals or an executable plan.

How Remarkable Women Lead reveals five common factors of the women interviewed in their study.[43]

1) Meaning: The sense of meaning is what inspires women leaders, guides their careers, sustains their optimism, generates positive emotions, and enables them to lead in creative and profound ways.

---

43 Joanna Barsh and Susie Cranston, *How Remarkable Women Lead: The Breakthrough Model for Work and Life* (New York: Crown Publishing, 2009), 10, 11.

2) Framing: To sustain herself on the path to leadership and to function as a leader, a woman must view situations clearly and avoid downward spirals in order to move ahead, adapt, and implement solutions.

3) Connecting: Nobody does it alone. Women leaders make meaningful connections to develop sponsorship and followership, to collaborate with colleagues and supporters with warmth and humanity.

4) Engaging: Successful leaders take ownership for opportunities along with risks. They have a voice, and they use it. They're also able to face down their fears.

5) Energizing: To succeed long-term and to accommodate family and community responsibilities, women leaders learn to manage their energy reserves and tap into flow.

Of the five successful contributing factors for women leaders, meaning outweighed all the others. Understanding what inspires us and what we are passionate about helps support all other areas, empowering us to lead in creative and insightful ways.

> Understanding what inspires us and what we are passionate about . . . empowers us to lead in creative and insightful ways.

Meaning in work and life dates back to ancient Greece: "In the fourth century B.C., Aristotle wrote that people achieve *eudaimonia* (a contented state of flourishing) when they fully use their unique talents, thereby fulfilling their basic function in life."[44]

Second Timothy 1:6 reminds us of meaning and passion: "For this reason I remind you to fan into flame the gift of God, which is in you through the laying on of hands." The field of positive psychology links meaningful activity with happiness:

Meaning is the motivation in your life. It's finding what engages you, what makes your heart beat faster, what gives you energy and creates passion. Meaning enables you to push yourself to the limit of your capabilities—and beyond.[45]

---

44 Barsh and Cranston, *How Remarkable Women Lead*, 21.

45 Barsh and Cranston, *How Remarkable Women Lead*, 22.

To help define meaning in your life, take a moment to answer a few questions:

- What are some of your core strengths? We all have them. Do you love to learn? Do you love justice? Are you creative? Analytical?
- What gives you a sense of purpose?
- What motivates you?
- What drains you of your energy?
- Does your work itself make you happy, regardless of the rewards or prestige?

As Gordon T. Smith notes in *Courage and Calling*:

> *When we speak of calling, we do so with the appreciation of the extraordinary potential of each person to make a difference for good. By this I do not mean that everyone needs to be a hero, but rather, in the midst of the simple ordinariness of everyday life, the work we do has the capacity to be good work that has profound worth and significance.*[46]

Without the realization of significance in every season of life, the stress of ministry overrides the individual's sense of self-worth and clouds how we understand calling. Emotional health and well-being are important in calling, but *meaning* contributes to the happiness factor. Studies show that "happiness is motivating, happier teams are more creative, leaders who exude happiness are more effective, and happiness improves physical health, as well as stamina and resilience."[47]

Jeremiah 1:5 states, "Before I formed you in the womb I knew you, before you were born I set you apart; I appointed you as a prophet to the nations." Identifying personal uniqueness, strengths, weaknesses, spiritual giftings, and passions will become clearer when we grow more dependent on the One who has formed us.

In *Strengthening the Soul of Your Leadership,* Ruth Haley Barton delivers this truth powerfully:

> *Vocation does not come from a voice "out there" calling me to be something I am not. It comes from a voice "in here" calling me to be the person I was born to be, to fulfill the original selfhood given to me at birth by God.*[48]

When leaders engage this truth into their daily practices of leadership, they entrust to the Creator rather than the creation their security about gifting, skills, and

46 Gordon T. Smith, *Courage and Calling: Embracing Your God-Given Potential* (Downers Grove, IL: InterVarsity Press, 2011), 19.

47 Barsh and Cranston, *How Remarkable Women Lead,* 24.

48 Ruth Haley Barton, *Strengthening the Soul of Your Leadership,* 77.

vision. Their hard work and striving surrenders to the all-knowing and all-powerful God; they then run this race with a restful stride.

Reflection Questions:

1) Review the five common factors of women who lead: meaning, framing, connecting, engaging, and energizing. Of the five, which one is lacking in your life? Which one comes easy for you in life and leadership?
2) Take some time to define meaning in your life by answering the core questions in this chapter:
3) What are some of your core strengths?
4) What gives you a sense of purpose?
5) What motivates you? What drains you of your energy?
6) Does your work itself make you happy, regardless of the rewards or prestige?

CHAPTER 10

IT'S ALL ABOUT YOU AND IT'S NOT ABOUT YOU AT ALL

"Listen carefully: Unless a grain of wheat is buried in the ground,
dead to the world, it is never any more than a grain of wheat. But if
it is buried, it sprouts and reproduces itself many times over."
—John 12:24 (MSG)

I wasn't a natural-born leader, not the "Who's Who" of the youth group. When I arrived on the Bible college campus I attended, I was insecure, homesick, unsure of myself, and scared. But I knew I was doing what God wanted me to do and that I was where He wanted me to be. I did not make choir (funny, because I would end up being a worship pastor) or travel with any ministry groups (this was a big deal). I often felt overlooked, and I was afraid to speak up in class.

I wasn't a natural-born leader, not the "Who's Who" of the youth group.

Everything changed one day when sitting in my missions class, where I remained strategically hidden for fear of being called on. The professor, David Wyns, shared about a class project that would be completed under the direction of five group leaders he would select.

As he called out those names, I was stunned that he chose me as one of the five class leaders. I thought, *No, I am not a leader. I am not the one. I have tried to stay hidden from the group so that I am not chosen. Is he not aware that I cannot do this?*

That evening as I contemplated my situation, I determined the only solution was to meet with the professor the next day and plead with him to let me step aside, so the group could be led by someone more capable. When the meeting took place, I came with a carefully written list of all the reasons why I should not be one of the leaders.

When I finished talking, I said, "Professor Wyns, you have picked the wrong person to lead the group."

He responded, "No, Lisa, I have picked the *right* person. You just don't know it yet."

Moses, at his burning bush experience, tried to give many convincing arguments to God as to why others would not follow him. The underlying truth for Moses, and for all of us, is that none of these reasons have substance in light of the One who calls:

> In this amazing dialogue Moses experienced the great paradox of calling: God is saying, in essence, it is all about you (because you are the one I have called) and it's not about you at all (because it was all about me and my work in and through you).[49]

The word *leading* has a variety of meanings: main, chief, prime, most significant, and most important. When compared to Jesus' leadership model, however, none of these words or phrases seem relevant. Jesus chose to wash feet before having His feet tended to. He taught a principle of the last being first and the first being last.

Can you imagine what a vision team meeting would look like with the early church team? Peter would have spoken up and said, "Hey, everyone, we are entrusted with this treasure—Jesus left the message with us, what should we do?"

Calling requires us to lead in following Christ, and part of that requirement means dying to self—taking up our cross to follow Jesus. Dying happens early in the calling process, and it happens continuously. I am a little like Peter when it comes

---

49 Barton, *Strengthening the Soul of Your Leadership*, 81.

to talk of dying—"All this talk of dying Lord—No!" But Jesus rebuked him and said, "Get thee behind me, Satan" (Luke 4:8, KJV). Death and dying will always remain part of the process.

Words such as *selfless*, *sacrificing*, *giving*, and *dying* are not often-used words—at least, not by me. The connotations of the words usually bring fear that someday God may hold me accountable for the weightiness of each word. This "dying to self" gospel and the "less of me and more of you" paradigm remains difficult to accept. Who wants to embrace hardship?

Embracing hardship and unwanted circumstances, however, is part of the process of dying to self. It can mean sickness, loss of a loved one, loss of finances, and unwillingness to forgive, transition, and so on. The reality remains that we need jostling out of our comfortable place to die to self and lead well.

In calling and leadership, you will experience many "dark nights of the soul," a poignant phrase written by the sixteenth-century priest and poet, St. John of the Cross. Jesus spoke to His disciples about the hard road they would travel. In referring to this, author David Platt writes:

> On another occasion, right after Jesus commended Peter for his confession of faith in him as "the Christ, the Son of the living God," Jesus rebuked Peter for missing the magnitude of what this means. Like many people today, Peter wanted a Christ without a cross and a Savior without any suffering. So Jesus looked at Peter and the other disciples and said, "If anyone would come after me, he must deny himself and take up his cross and follow me. For whoever wants to save his life will lose it, but whoever loses his life for me will find it."[50]

The leading to follow call means having the willingness to go to the hard places, do the hard things, and allow discomfort in life for the sake of the gospel—taking up one's cross and following Him, wherever this may lead and whatever the cost. For the original disciples, it cost their lives.

In July 2014, my family faced the reality of death with kingdom purpose when my brother died on a missions trip to India. The accident occurred while he, along with men from his church and the missionary, trekked through the Himalayas to share the gospel.

---

50 David Platt, *Follow Me: A Call to Die. A Call to Live* (Carol Stream, IL: Tyndale House Publishers, Inc., 2013), 11.

After his death, the missionary recounted a story about Terry that happened a few days earlier. They met at base camp to review a list of helpful rules to follow for relating to the people and understanding their culture.

At the end of the session, Terry approached the missionary privately and said, "At the end of this trip, I'm going to give you another one to add to your list." The missionary shared with us later that while he and two other men carried his body on a make-shift stretcher to a nearby village, the thought occurred to him that Terry had written rule number eleven: *It may cost your life, but are you willing to go?* The idea that you or I will experience literal death for the cause of Christ is unlikely, but Jesus speaks of a spiritual principle that leaders cannot ignore—dying to self. Leaders must take up their cross and follow Jesus. They must lead to follow. While this usually does not make sense, it remains a practice that leaders must apply.

> The idea that you or I will experience literal death for the cause of Christ is unlikely, but Jesus speaks of a spiritual principle that leaders cannot ignore–dying to self.

The reciprocal part of calling happens in death. John 12:24 states that "unless a kernel of wheat falls to the ground and dies, it remains only a single seed. But if it dies, it produces many seeds."

Reflection Questions:

1) Is there a place in your calling that you are insecure, unsure, or afraid?
2) Take some time to pray about this matter, and allow God to speak into your life about the reasons why you feel insecure or afraid.
3) Have you had a burning-bush moment? If so, write about it or share it with a friend.

CHAPTER 11
VISION AND VALUES

And he will be like a tree firmly planted [and fed] by streams of
water, which yields its fruit in its season; its leaf does not wither; and
in whatever he does, he prospers [and comes to maturity].
—Psalm1:3 (AMP)

We are almost to the end of our calling journey. I hope you are working on your vision and values statement and enjoying the discovery of what brings you meaning and the passions that cause you to flourish.

Paul writes, "We pray for you all the time—pray that our God will make you fit for what he's called you to be, pray that he'll fill your good ideas and acts of faith with his own energy so that it all amounts to something" (2 Thessalonians 1:11, MSG). I am praying for you, and as you lead from this humble posture, I know that God is filling your good ideas with acts of faith so that your work amounts to much more than you could ever imagine.

I would like to introduce one more exercise to use as a guide. It is a Personal Inventory and Growth Plan. I suggest developing the plan to cover three months and then revisit it again after the three months have passed.

Embrace the idea that God longs to mentor you.

The plan is developed from "an exercise in listening prayer (not self-improvement) and intentional cooperation (not self-direction)."[51] As you listen, contemplate, and embrace the idea that God longs to mentor you.

(Appendix D)

Personal Inventory and Growth Plan:

Dates: _____

Spiritual	Physical	Family	Ministry	Sabbath/ Rest
Student of the Word. Begin studying a chapter or book in the Bible. Incorporate memorization and journaling. Student of Prayer. Create times of listening to God, being still. Utilize mornings for study and prayer.	Get healthier. Healthy eating: Eliminate most sugars from diet. More fruits and vegetables. Exercise: Strive for 30 minutes, 5 days a week.			

Measure your journey on this growth plan by recognizing God's presence in your life—from a heaven-down, not earth-up perspective. Earth-up evaluation looks at performance and checks off a to-do list. The heaven-down approach asks God how *He* thinks you are doing, whether your life aligns with His purposes more than it did before you started, and whether you remain more aware of keeping a sabbath. This heaven-down approach seeks a response from the question, "God, what do you see?" Think through what resources you will need for your growth plan.

51 Alicia Britt Chole, "Movement Two: Toward Intentionality, Week Eight," *The 7th Year*, March 16, 2015, www.the7thyear.com.

As you complete the vision/value statements and personal inventory/growth plan, think of the stages of life. For those of you in early to middle adulthood, it is a time in which you establish yourself in the world. For most of you, this will be the time to start a career and possibly a family. We also begin to ask the basic question about our identity: *Who am I, in the middle of all this?*

At this point we have decisions to make about our strengths, our desires, our temperament, and what brings the fullest expression of who we are. "It is probably fair to say that we do not really know ourselves until our mid-thirties, which is why we cannot make the transition to mid-adulthood—full adulthood—until this time.

"Clarity for vocational purposes can only come after we have lived with ourselves long enough to be able to ask, for example, what matters to me more than anything else?"[52] Maybe you are gifted in many different areas and that makes decisions much harder. It takes discernment and learning to say *no* to some things and *yes* to others.

If we are not careful, these decisions can yield disorder and anxiety. That is why the exercises I have included in this step are helpful in defining who you are. I have found that I express myself differently over time, but who I am has been rather consistent with my core-self.

Surrender to God your insecurities
about your calling and lean in to
hear how He affirms you.

Invest some time in closing out this section by reviewing your vision and values statements. Reflect and be grateful for who you are, and the passions God has put in your heart. Surrender to God your insecurities about your calling and lean in to hear how He affirms you.

---

52 Gordon T. Smith, *Courage and Calling*, 85.

Reflection Questions:

1) How could practicing and living in a heaven-down approach change your life?

2) Do you struggle from anxiety at times? If so, what do you think the root is? Is it perfection? Is it over committing? Is it insecurity?

3) What matters to you more than anything?

PART FOUR

COMMUNITY: THE POWER OF YOUR NETWORK

Wounds from a friend can be trusted, but an enemy multiplies kisses.
—Proverbs 27:6

Welcome to the fourth and final foundation in *The Collective Journey*—Community: The Power of Your Network. The outward-focused step is rooted in the number one struggle faced by female leaders—loneliness. Women often remain excluded from the table of male leaders while dealing with rejection from other women who, in their own biases, fail to understand how calling is not gender specific.

The important role of community in one's life cannot be diluted.

The important role of community in one's life cannot be diluted. Jesus exemplified the love of community: "Having loved his own who were in the world, he loved them to the end" (John 13:1). Women must not compromise community.

"To compromise community would be to compromise our essence and then we would not have much that is of value to offer to others."[53]

An old African proverb says, "If you want to travel fast, travel alone; if you want to travel far, travel together." To enhance this point and conclude this last foundation, you will take an assessment tool from *Habitudes* on relationships.[54] The assessment looks at six different types of community: models—people who do what you do; heroes—people you look up to and admire; mentors—people who coach you and invest in you; partners—people who travel with you and hold you accountable; inner circle—those who are closest to you, like family and close friends; and mentees—people who learn from you.[55] You do not need to fill every blank on the assessment, but you should prayerfully seek the individuals who can become a part of your trusted community.

C. S. Lewis once said, "Friendship is born at that moment when one person says to another, 'What! You too? I thought I was the only one.'"[56] Lisa McKay notes the value of friendship: "There is an instant bonding when we know we are not alone in our passions and pains."[57] A trusted community shares the power of our story and realizes that we are not alone on the leadership journey.

Even Jesus had those with whom He intimately shared the journey. He created community with the twelve disciples, allowing Peter, James, and John into His inner circle and disclosing all of His heart to God, His Father. In the last foundation, community, you will gratefully uncover any lack or abundance of existing community and then prayerfully build a stronger community that will assist you in your personal and leadership life.

Community Assessment
- Review and complete assessment on Relationship Resource Page. (Appendix I)
- Develop a better understanding of community and how it relates to our relationship in Christ.

---

53 Barton, *Strengthening the Soul*, 176.

54 Tim Elmore and Harvey Herman, *Habitudes: Images That Form Leadership Habits and Attitudes* (Atlanta, GA: Growing Leaders, Inc., 2013), 17.

55 Elmore and Herman, *Habitudes*, 17.

56 Lisa McKay, *You Can Still Wear Cute Shoes* (Colorado Springs: CO: David C. Cook, 2010), 95.

57 McKay, *You Can Still Wear Cute Shoes*, 95.

■ With gratitude, uncover any abundance or lack in your existing community and then prayerfully build a stronger community that will assist you in your personal and leadership life.

Living It Out Rhythms–Community

Table 4. Foundation Four: Community

COMMUNITY	COMMUNITY	COMMUNITY	COMMUNITY
Soulful You	Mindful You	Heartful You	Creative You
This spiritual retreat or sabbath day should be taken with a friend or mentor. Make sure it's life-giving. Thank God for this connection.	Do a study on friend or mentor relationships in the Bible, such as Jonathan and David, Naomi and Ruth, or Paul, Timothy, and Titus.	Send some thank you cards to a few of the people on your Relationship Resource Page and tell them how grateful you are that they have impacted your life. Be specific.	Make some cards to send for your *Heartful You* Rhythm. Use craft supplies or print photos of yourself and the person you are sending the thank you note to. This will be another reminder of how others have impacted your life.

Community Book Suggestions

Brown, Brené. *Braving the Wilderness: The Quest for True Belonging and the Courage to Stand Alone.* New York: Random House, 2017.

CHAPTER 12

YOU WERE CREATED
FOR COMMUNITY

I lift up my eyes to the hills. From where does my help [ezer] *come? My help* [ezer] *comes from the Lord, the Maker of heaven and earth.*
—Psalm 121:1-2 (BSB)

I was twenty-eight years old with two small children. We had relocated to a new ministry where everything was different. This was already my third church where I would serve as pastor's wife. I had carried hurts from the previous places of ministry; the sadness and the shell I had built around my heart sheltered me from the sweet people who tried to be my friends.

At some point in my obviously depressed state, my husband and I decided I needed to see a counselor, someone who could help me move past the junk and guide me to healing the hurts. As I sat in the waiting room of the counselor's office, I was much more broken than I realized at that moment.

I poured my heart out (yes, *poured* it out and cried all over myself). The counselor listened intently and offered several suggestions. At the end, when I thought he would say something profound to make it all go away, he looked at me and said, "Lisa, who are your friends?" I sat quietly and I could not think of one person, not one friend. He was kind in his approach, but he said to me, "Your homework assignment this week is to find a friend."

On the ride home, I came up with every reason as to why I couldn't find a friend, especially with a one-week timeline. I pulled into the driveway of our home and bowed my head and prayed this prayer: *Dear God, I can't do this without You. Please guide me to a friend, one to whom I can entrust my heart.* The next day, the morning began with a routine school drop-off with the children. Andrew needed a permission slip signed, so I stepped inside the hallway of the small Christian school they attended. I was feeling the heaviness of my counseling appointment from the day before when I headed back to the car for an ordinary day at home.

As I exited the building, two women, new to our church and school, asked what I was doing for the morning and whether I would like to join them for coffee. Stunned by their question, I wondered if the two women standing in front of me were answers to my prayer.

That day we shared more than coffee as the Holy Spirit opened our hearts to one another. Ann, Naomi, and I have an inner-circle friendship that remains strong twenty-five years later. I am a better leader today because of their friendship and influence in my life.

My point is simple—you cannot take a short-cut on community. To align everything else in the leadership journey, checking off the boxes, and having the right credentials will not make you a great leader. Sustainable leadership finds its place in community.

Sustainable leadership finds its place in community.

Loneliness is often the number-one struggle for female leaders. The loneliness we feel as leaders can often set us up for other unhealthy leadership practices: "When we feel isolated, disconnected, and lonely, we try to protect ourselves. In that mode, we want to connect, but our brain is attempting to override connection with self-protection. That means less empathy, more defensiveness, more numbing, and less sleeping."[58]

The lack of community, support network, and disconnecting from friendships results in weakness and vulnerability. Leadership brings with it busy lives, and often the time constraints of developing and maintaining close relationships stand in the way, but Brown conveys that "numerous studies confirm that it's not the quantity of friends but the quality of a few relationships that actually matter."[59]

Jesus modeled the principle well with how He spoke to the crowds, how He discipled the Twelve, His close relationship with the inner circle (Peter, James, and John), and how He spoke everything to God in prayer. If Jesus needed to have others go with Him on the journey, how much more do *we* need community along the way? When it came time for Jesus to do what He needed to do alone—death on the cross—He was prepared.

Without getting into a lengthy study on the Hebrew words *ezer-kenegdo*, it remains important to note the correlation between community and the creation of the woman. Genesis 2:22 says:

> *Then the Lord God made woman from the rib he had taken out of the man, and he brought her to the man. The man said, "This is now bone of my bones and flesh of my flesh; she shall be called 'woman,' for she was taken out of man."*

The word *ezer* used for "woman" literally means "half." *Kenegdo* means "suitable." The Hebrew word *ezer* in the masculine tense is used twenty-one times in the Old Testament and more often refers to God Himself: "I lift up my eyes to the hills. From where does my help [*ezer*] come? My help [*ezer*] comes from the Lord, the Maker of heaven and earth" (Psalm 121:1-2, BSB). In Deuteronomy, *ezer* is used three times as a military term—the cavalry that comes, the battle that cannot be won until the reinforcements show up. Daniel refers to *ezer* as the help that is necessary to overcome the times of persecution.

---

58 Brené Brown, *Braving the Wilderness: The Quest for True Belonging and the Courage to Stand Alone* (New York: Random House, 2017), 54-55.

59 Brown, *Braving the Wilderness*, 55.

> It doesn't take much imagination to
> see how God created the essence of
> our femaleness to come alongside,
> to help, to be reinforcement.

It doesn't take much imagination to see how God created the essence of our femaleness to come alongside, to help, to be reinforcement. You were made for community. Our help and suitability root us in the likeness of God, our Creator.

Reflection Questions:

1) If loneliness is often the number one struggle for female leaders, how have you noticed a lonely leadership path in your own journey?

2) What traits of isolation do you currently have or have had in the past?
   - Defensiveness
   - Lack of empathy
   - Self-protection
   - Lack of sleep

3) Begin reflecting on your community/network. Do you have an inner circle of friends? Do you have a larger group of individuals who hold you accountable and cheer for you?

CHAPTER 13

YOU BELONG TO A TRIBE
MUCH BIGGER THAN YOU

"This is my command: Love one another the way I loved you. This
is the very best way to love. Put your life on the line for your friends.
You are my friends when you do the things, I command you."
—John 15:11-12 (MSG)

As women, the very idea of who we are and how God created us speaks of community. We are created for tribal living. In the 1970s, there was a movie titled *Tribes* that used the term in sense of a closely bonded group of individuals who share a common culture. The movies and TV have helped to promote the use of the term "tribe" to reflect a social group that shares a common culture, and it has drifted into being a substitute for the term "community" for some people.

A suitable helper is not walking behind,
or in front of, but is coming alongside.

In the last chapter, I talked about the idea that we are *ezer-kenegdo* which means a suitable helper. The suitable helper is not walking behind, or in front of, but is coming alongside.

I remember the moment I realized my tribe was much bigger than me. My grandparents had a large garden, and every summer when it was time to harvest the strawberries, blueberries, tomatoes, green beans, peas, potatoes, corn, and so on, we (the women) would gather in Grandma's kitchen and front porch to begin canning, freezing, making jelly, homemade ketchup, and other goodies that my grandma learned from being raised on a farm.

My mom and her sister were the only siblings, and there were only two granddaughters, myself and my cousin Beverly. I was the youngest of the grandchildren, so someone was always trying to protect me or teach me how to do something. The day had come when, according to my grandmother, I would "put up the corn."

Putting up the corn required handling hot ears of corn that had been precooked and sharp knives for cutting the corn off the cob. I had finally graduated to using a knife. The concern around the kitchen, for the entire day, was about me handling the knife and being careful not to cut my fingers.

Aunt Shirley, Mom, Grandma, and Bev watched me carefully throughout the day. They corrected me when I needed it and cheered for me when I managed to put up my first dozen ears of corn and place them in the freezer bags. We didn't high-five then, but a sweet little shoulder squeeze from Grandma and a nodding smile from the others helped me to know that the family I belonged to are my tribe, and they cheer me on to succeed.

The Proverbs 31 passage is often viewed as an exhausting checklist of items that women cannot accomplish, whether in one day, one week, or one year. Proverbs 31 is an acrostic poem. The subject of this twenty-two-line poem, the "woman of noble character," is meant to be a tangible expression of the book's celebrated virtue of wisdom. It essentially shows us what wisdom looks like in practical ways.

In Jewish culture, it is not the woman who memorizes Proverbs 31, but the men. They memorize it to sing it as a song of praise to the women in their lives—their wives, daughters, sisters, mothers, and friends. It is usually sung every Sabbath meal at the Shabbat feast. Notably, the only instructive language in the poem is directed at the poem's intended male audience: "Praise her for all her hands have done."

The first line of the Proverbs 31 poem, "A virtuous woman who can find?" is best translated as "A woman of valor who can find?" The Hebrew word used for "virtuous and woman of valor" is *eschet chayil.* The Hebrew phrase, *eschet chayil,* is used in Jewish culture to cheer one another on with the blessing of celebrating everything from promotions, to pregnancies, to acts of mercy and justice, to battles with cancer with a hearty, "Eschet chayil!" Think about it as not what you do, but how you do it and who you are. If you're a stay-at-home mom, be a stay-at-home mom of valor. If you're a nurse, be a nurse of valor. If you are a CEO, a pastor, a barista at Starbucks . . . if you are rich, poor, single, or married, do it with valor.

Here is the key point: *eschet chayil* women of valor do a lot of high-fiving. In our culture it would be equivalent to saying, "You go, girl!" The problem occurs, however, when women leaders do not set up a culture of cheering.

The "You go, girl" culture has to begin somewhere. So, why not you? Why not me?

All of us have experienced the jealously, discouraging comments, and older female leaders telling us, "You're young, and it is not your time yet." The "You go, girl" culture has to begin somewhere. So, why not *you?* Why not *me?*

A functional family gives you the knife and your one dozen ears of corn and watches you carefully so that you will succeed. You were made for tribal living, for community, and your tribe is cheering you on.

Reflection Questions:

1) Journal about a time when you felt cheered for and then think about a time that you didn't receive a high five or "Well done!"

2) Thank God for the men in your life who declare you as a woman of valor. Take some time to study Proverbs 31 and the eschet chayil of cheering you on.

CHAPTER 14

YOUR TRIBE CONNECTS YOU TO OTHER TRIBES (TRIBES ARE GENERATIONAL)

The Lord announces the word, and the women who proclaim it are a mighty throng.
—Psalm 68:11

As I previously mentioned in the beginning of the book, several years ago, I participated in a pre-conference prayer retreat. After the speaker had given a brief devotion, she encouraged the group to find a place to listen and pray. I found a spot in the back of the room and positioned myself on the floor with my Bible, journal, and pen.

As the music played softly in the background, I closed my eyes to focus my hearing. Within several minutes, I began sensing that God wanted to reveal something significant. I picked up my Bible and journal and turned to Psalms, finding a passage I had not seen before: "The Lord announces the word, and the women who proclaim it are a mighty throng" (68:11). Stunned, I picked up my journal and began to write: *God is getting ready to raise up a mighty army of women who are full of the Spirit.* Although the revelation of what God showed me that day was significant, the larger revelation would come later on as I further studied Psalm 68:11. The meaning of the phrase "the word" in verse 11 is the same meaning that appears in Psalm 19:4, "Yet their voice goes out into all the earth, their words to the ends of the world." The meaning of the "words" in each scripture is "divine utterance"—"The Lord announces the *divine utterance*, and the women who proclaim it are a mighty throng" (emphasis mine.)

In other words, the women proclaim what they hear from God. The Lord's voice goes out to the ends of the earth by the women declaring it.

The Lord's voice goes out to the ends of the earth by the women declaring it.

In the Old Testament during declarations of victory, women possessed the responsibility of celebrating a triumph. Women expressed these victorious declarations through songs and dance. An example of this appears in Exodus 15:20-21, when Miriam begins to sing:

When Pharaoh's horses, chariots and horsemen went into the sea, the Lord brought the waters of the sea back over them, but the Israelites walked through the sea on dry ground. Then Miriam the prophet, Aaron's sister, took the timbrel in her hand and all the women followed her, with timbrels and dancing. Miriam sang to them, "Sing to the Lord for he is highly exalted. Both the horse and driver he has hurled into the sea."

Again, Judges 5 features the Song of Deborah. In verse 7, Deborah sings, "Villagers in Israel would not fight; they held back, until, I, Deborah, arose, until I arose, a mother in Israel." Both passages illustrate the teaching of successive generations.

Miriam started singing, and the women and their daughters followed her. As leaders, they stepped up to teach both their community and the generations. Further, Deborah's obedience gave her the title of Mother of Israel. Mother is a generational term. Not to sound silly but a mother has a mother and she has a child.

Generations continue through motherhood, growing the tribe. Tribes are a generational connection. Deborah acted as a mother to Israel. Appointed as the judge of Israel, she allowed her femaleness to shine through her leadership. When the battle was won, she made a song declaration. She acted as *ezer*, a warrior, the help that Israel needed. Tribes speak of the passing of traditions from one generation to another.

The precedent of women celebrating the victory means they did not simply celebrate one victory, but successive victories. Such declarations did not come from one large body of women celebrating one specific victory, but multiple women over many generations. They celebrated each successive victory, rapidly, one after another and another and another.

By developing community, a tribe, a successive multi-generational community, you develop the sense that you belong to something bigger than yourself, with the older teaching the younger and the younger teaching the older. Such collaboration remains uniquely feminine: "I hate stereotypes, but as I have watched female and male leaders, it seems to be the instinctive preference of women to bring everybody along."[60]

Why not use the instinctive preference of bringing everyone along to your advantage and embrace a growing tribe of unique, wonder-filled, strong women who join to link arms and walk shoulder to shoulder to fulfill God's call on their lives? I remind you of the African proverb: "If you want to travel fast, travel alone; if you want to travel far, travel together."

> Why not use the instinctive preference of bringing everyone along to your advantage and embrace a growing tribe of unique, wonder-filled, strong women who join to link arms and walk shoulder to shoulder to fulfill God's call on their lives?

Reflection Questions:

1) Take some time to retreat and finish the "My Network" page.
2) Look at the places where you have blanks and pray that God would help you to fill those areas.

---

60 Joanna Barsh and Susie Cranston, *How Remarkable Women Lead*, 182.

CHAPTER 15

HEAVEN-DOWN
AND EARTH-UP

"Keep company with me and you'll learn to live freely and lightly."
—Matthew 11:30 (MSG)

Wow, you have almost made it to the end of *The Collective Journey*. As you have walked the path toward the inner and outer foundations of core-self, communion, calling, and community, you have realized and understood a lot of your life and leadership. Women grow stronger through being together; this proves especially true when women connect intergenerationally and learn from one another. Closing the gaps in generational leadership relies on successfully passing the baton of leadership. If the baton drops, however, gaps will appear and women will suffer from a lack of leadership development.

Identifying and mentoring female leaders who are secure in their calling, belong to a meaningful community, share their stories to create change, and seek leadership development will enhance the pipeline with strong, capable female leaders.

To conclude *The Collective Journey*, there are three more paths we must take to understand the work that the Holy Spirit is doing in our lives up to this point—the journey of laying down perfectionism, passing on our dreams, and taking a seat at the table. All three are crucial to the full-circle pathway of connecting the generations in wholeness of life and leadership. They each flow from a rich place of congruency in the inner and outer world of a leader.

Perfectionism is relentless and exhausting.

Nearly everyone struggles with perfectionism. Maybe my need to believe that everyone struggles with perfectionism helps me feel better about the daily battle I experience to get off the perfectionist merry-go-round. Perfectionism is relentless and exhausting. It isolates, highlights inferiority, produces shame, and creates a false-self.

Although a clear-cut definition of perfectionism remains difficult to communicate, explaining what perfectionism *is not* is a bit easier: "Perfectionism is not the same thing as striving to be your best. Perfectionism is not self-improvement."[61]

It is important to work toward healthy achievement and growth. Perfectionism creates a false-self, one that believes that the false-self will somehow give way to all we desire. At its core, perfectionism tries to earn acceptance and approval.

In striving for perfection, we settle with "I wish" rather than "I'm grateful," when assessing ourselves.

Perfectionism and the hunt for perfection ruins lives, leaving us incapable of seeing ourselves from a heaven-downward perspective, especially in a culture in which achievements and wealth speak of success. Living in the daily shadow of perfection makes the end of the day, the end of the project, or the end of the journey look unmet and half-hearted. In striving for perfection, we settle with "I wish" rather than "I'm grateful," when assessing ourselves.

I have come to realize that the greatest trap in our life is not success, popularity, or power but self-rejection. Success, popularity, and power can indeed present a great temptation, but their seductive quality often comes from the

---

61 Brené Brown, *The Gifts of Imperfection: Let Go of Who You Think You're Supposed to Be and Embrace Who You Are* (Center City, MN: Hazelden Publishing, 2010), 56.

way they are part of the much larger temptation of self-rejection. When we have come to believe in the voices that call us worthless and unlovable, then success, popularity, and power are easily perceived as attractive solutions. The real trap, however, is self-rejection. . . . Self-rejection is the greatest enemy of the spiritual life because it contradicts the sacred voice that calls us "Beloved." Being the Beloved constitutes the core truth of our existence.[62]

Living with a heaven-downward perspective means living in a space that helps us realize, at the end of everything, we remain God's beloved, and unmet goals or performance will not change that truth. Heaven-downward assessment always views achievements in light of to Whom we belong:

> *It used to be that I never felt safe with myself unless I was performing flaw-lessly. My desire to be perfect was greater than my desire for God. Bullied by an all-or-nothing standard of my own making, I interpreted weakness as mediocrity and inconsistency as a loss of nerve. I thought compassion and self-acceptance were self-indulgent. Eventually I just wore myself out. My sense of personal failure and inadequacy stripped my self-esteem bare, triggering episodes of mild depression and wild anxiety. The desire to be perfect was greater than my desire for God.*[63]

Performing a task well, striving to do your best, self-improvement, and having a life well-lived is not the issue. God expects us to give our best. When our best is still not good enough and the burden of perfectionism turns into a false-self, then we have traded our beloved status for an earthly reward that will diminish the heavenly perspective. To say no to perfection is saying yes to presence. A heaven-downward approach remains open-hearted, not heavy-hearted.

The trap of living an unhealthy life centered on perfection remains a strong temptation in the life of a leader. Scazzero talks about three such temptations that aid the false-self: I am what I do (performance); I am what I have (possession); and I am what others think (popularity).[64] Instead of holding onto these lies, we are invited to keep company with Jesus and take the risk that God's intentions toward us are good: "Keep company with me and you'll learn to live freely and lightly" (Matthew 11:30, MSG).

---

62 Henri J. M. Nouwen, *Life of the Beloved* (New York: Crossroad, 1992), 21.

63 Brennan Manning and Jim Hancock, *Posers, Fakers, & Wannabes: Unmasking the Real You* (Colorado Springs, CO: NavPress, 2003), 30-31.

64 Peter Scazzero, *Emotionally Healthy Spirituality,* 75-77.

Reflection Questions:

1) How do we keep perfectionism from interrupting our endeavors?
2) How would you view the last six months of the mentoring journey from a perfectionistic approach?
3) How would you view the last six months of the mentoring journey from a heaven-downward approach? As the Beloved?
4) What does "in the present" look like in your future life journey?

CHAPTER 16

THE PASSING ON
OF DREAMS

*"The Lord bless you and keep you; the Lord make his face shine on you and
be gracious to you; the Lord turn his face toward you and give you peace."*
—Numbers 6:24-26

The Harvard School of Business narrows the leadership journey to one statement: "Leadership is about making others better as a result of your presence and making sure that impact lasts in your absence." In other words, leadership is about building bridges. Responsibility for the next generation does not end.

Leadership is a reciprocal process that builds a bridge between the generation that went before and the generations that follow. The charge to show up and make a difference by being in the room and leaving tangible evidence that you were there long after you are gone is a tangible aspect of leading well.

I married a dreamer who turned me into a dreamer. When we first got married, I was often fearful of dreaming. It felt more secure to allow my life to reside in a neatly kept box. Thirty-five plus years later, dreaming days with Frank are my best days. He has taught me how to dream.

Our dream days probably would sound silly to some people if they listened to our dream day conversations. Others might say, "Listen to them. That will never happen," or "What time they waste on foolish dreams when they should be getting things done today." I agree that we must balance tasks and dreams. All dreams and no work, of course, will not make the dream a reality. All work and no allotted time for dreaming means a boring and mundane life.

Recently, in my daily Bible reading, I came across a passage about dreams in 1 Kings 8:17-19, when Solomon, David's son, completed the temple in Jerusalem:

> *My father David had it in his heart to build a temple for the Name of the LORD, the God of Israel. But the LORD said to my father David, "You did well to have it in your heart to build a temple for my Name. Nevertheless, you are not the one to build the temple, but your son, your own flesh and blood—he is the one who will build the temple for my Name." The story reveals that David received a "Well done!" from God by simply having it in his heart to build a temple. David was credited for doing well by having his dreams. Passing his dreams on to the generation coming after him released the promise that his dreams would be fulfilled.*

In other words, we have permission to dream, my friends! The Lord commended David for having the dream in his heart, and the commendation shows the importance God gives to dreams. Discernment and release of our dreams remain significant for leaders and the leaders they raise up. A responsibility awaits both the dreamer and the receiver of the dream. Ownership can be a tricky component. Do I want to be the hero or a hero-maker?

A responsibility awaits both the dreamer and the receiver of the dream. Ownership can be a tricky component. Do I want to be the hero or a hero-maker?

Matters of the heart always come into play when we struggle to release something of value. Our God-given dreams are valuable. We can only wonder whether the receiver of our dreams will treasure them and see their importance in the way that we did.

For those passing on their dreams, several perspectives should be practiced:

- Have open palms, not closed fists. The fulfillment of the dream must be more important to you than the dream. Your reward was in keeping the dream, while someone else is rewarded for the stewardship and fulfillment of the dream.
- Practice vulnerability and transparency. An open heart allows the conveyance of dreams to the next generation.
- Release the dream.

The passing on of dreams should be expected like the anticipated generational blessing. At the heart of parenting and leadership is a reward or blessing: "The Lord bless you and keep you; the Lord make his face shine on you and be gracious to you; the Lord turn his face toward you and give you peace" (Numbers 6:24-26).

The passing on of dreams should be expected like the anticipated generational blessing.

Conversely, if the older generation hoards their dreams with closed fists, the younger generation will eventually rebound and move forward. But think about the foundation that could have been laid for them with the blessing of dreams! Spiritual parenting conveys an inheritance of dreams, and children should expect an impartation of parental dreams to them. Your tribe is bigger than you. Your tribe includes generation, after generation, after generation. Each generation must cultivate the expectation to receive a bucketful of dreams.

Reflection Questions:

1) Journal about building bridges with the generation before and the one coming after you?
2) What is significant about these relationships? Do you gain wisdom and insight from them? Are you able to dream with them?
3) If dreaming isn't a part of your everyday life and leadership journey, start a dream journal this week and begin noting your dreams. As you write your dreams, remind yourself of David's "well done" for simply having dreams in his heart.

CHAPTER 17
AN INVITATION TO THE TABLE

"But when you give a banquet, invite the poor, the crippled, the lame, the blind, and you will be blessed. Although they cannot repay you, you will be repaid at the resurrection of the righteous."
—Luke 14: 13-14

Usually, the people we love most take up places at our tables. Meals are shared, stories told, sins confessed, laughing, and crying together. We are dreamers at my family table—thinking about where we have been and where we might one day go. We pray at the table, and at the table, we experience the kindness, grace, and mercy of God.

Sharing tables is one of the most human things we can do. Think about it. No other creature consumes its food at the table (although my golden retriever, Brady, would love an invitation to partake at our table).

I'm more apt to sit the food on the kitchen counter and let everyone scoop from the pot or dish in a hurried and busy life. Not my mom; she puts a tablecloth on the table and adds the plates, napkins, and silverware. She then dishes the food she prepared into beautiful bowls and sits them around the table. As we sit down to partake, a feeling of peace always comes over me, and I feel blessed to be a part of her family. It is a blessing that she would take the time to prepare a beautiful meal for me. I am convinced that one of my mom's delicious meals would bring world peace—especially if she made a lemon meringue pie.

> It shouldn't surprise us that God has a way of showing up at tables throughout the Bible.

We're often most fully alive when we are sharing a meal around the table. So it shouldn't surprise us that God has a way of showing up at tables throughout the Bible. At the center of our spiritual lives in the Old and New Testaments, we find the Passover table and the Communion table.

N. T. Wright makes a valuable point, "When Jesus himself wanted to explain to his disciples what his forthcoming death was all about, he didn't give them a theory; he gave them a meal."[65] I love this thought. It reminds me that we may need to discover the art of hospitality again to share the significant burdens and joys of our lives around our tables of food.

At our first Collective Journey closing retreat, I created a beautiful table for our group to sit at and share a meal. I chose a beautiful tablecloth, silver chargers, plates, linen napkins with gold napkin holders, flowers for centerpieces, individually wrapped gifts, and, at the last minute, I added place cards at each seat with the participants' names on them.

Little did I know the emotional and spiritual significance of this beautifully prepared table. So many beautiful women of God were seated at the table. Each one had a seat with her name on it. Each one belonged. The next day during her prayer retreat time, Stacy wrote about the table I had prepared for them.

A Seat at the Table (Stacy Eubanks)

It was a Thursday afternoon, and I arrived at the retreat house after scrambling to get everything done before a busy mom in ministry could leave town. My teenage

---

65 N. T. Wright, "Saving the World, Revealing the Glory: Atonement Then and Now," *ABC Religion and Ethics*, accessed September 20, 2021, https://www.abc.net.au/religion/saving-the-world-revealing-the-glory-atonement-then-and-now/10095866.

daughter was a hot mess, and I felt like a failure for so many reasons, but I had committed to this event, and I knew I needed to be there.

When I walked into the room, my eyes fell on a long table set for dinner. The table, thoughtfully and delightfully decorated with silver chargers, pretty plates, gleaming flatware, sparkling glasses, cheerful yellow pansies placed carefully as centerpieces, and an elegantly wrapped gift at every place setting.

I was carrying so much baggage when I got there that all I could think was, *Oh, my, I am not dressed for dinner at this table, and I packed so quickly that I don't even have anything nice to put on. But, I'm sure everyone won't fit anyway, so I will grab a seat at the bar nearby when it's time.*

And then I saw them. There were name cards at every place. I had never had a seat at the table with my name on it. But there it was, already reserved for me. I didn't feel worthy, but there *I* was, taking my place at a table prepared for me. That made me think about another table over two thousand years ago, perhaps the most significant table in all of history.

Doubters, deniers, and even betrayers, Jesus included them all at the table of the Passover.

Who got a seat at that table? Doubters, deniers, and even betrayers, Jesus included them all at the table of the Passover. He welcomed them despite what they had done and what He knew they would do. Thomas later doubted Him. Peter scoffed at Jesus' prediction of his denial of Him and denied Jesus only a few short hours after that last supper.

When Peter's eyes met those of Jesus, he was devastated at his failure. How could he be worthy of the bread Jesus had offered, but it was provided, nonetheless. And Judas? Really? How did *he* merit a seat at the table?? Of course, he didn't, but he had one anyway.

Jesus passed the bread of His body and the cup of His blood to a traitor with a heart filled with darkness. Yet, He offered love and forgiveness down to the last second.

And what about me? I am a doubter, a denier, AND a betrayer. So how is it that I am allowed at the table? I can't buy a seat with my righteousness. Apart from Christ, I have none.

I'm allowed at the table for one reason only: Jesus bought my seat. He paid for it in blood and reserved my place. He has saved a seat for you too. There is a card with your name on it and a gift waiting for you. Are you coming?

It's a table where paupers become princes, losers become leaders, failures are forgiven, and the wretched are redeemed. So don't worry about what to wear or what to bring; do whatever it takes to get to the table. And come hungry! There is nothing more satisfying than the table He has prepared for you.[66]

We Gather Blessed, Broken, Forgiven, and Not Yet Forgiven

At the beginning of *The Collective Journey,* I introduced the spiritual discipline of prayer retreating. To complete the journey, I want to acquaint you with the art of table fellowship—a gathering place for the blessed, broken, forgiven, and the not yet forgiven.

As Stacy wrote about her experience at the table, she recalled how she had the feeling that she didn't belong and didn't bring the right clothes to sit at the table— every excuse that came her way because she didn't belong. But when she took her seat—the place with her name on the place card—she let go of shame and insecurity and accepted the blessing of being invited to the table.

Brokenness shows up at the table. Jesus made the Samaritan well a table when He spoke to the woman about her broken life and gave her the answer to her most profound shame. "Come, see a man who told me everything I ever did. Could this be the Messiah?" (John 4:29) This statement came from a heart truly set free. While going to retrieve water, a woman met the Living Water and drank from a well where the water never runs dry.

We set the table for the forgiven and the not yet forgiven. I love the restoration picture that John 21 illustrates. The image of Jesus, the Son of God, fixing breakfast for His disciples gives me goosebumps on my goosebumps.

---

66 Stacy Eubanks, "A Seat at the Table," *Women Who Lead Blog,* https://www.pmnwomenwholead.com/blog/aseatatthetable.

We set the table for the forgiven and the not yet forgiven.

This table prepared on the Sea of Galilee is not simply a meal to eat for the stomach's sake; it is a meal of reestablishing a relationship between Peter and Jesus. It is a place where food leads the way to forgiveness.

In this passage, the word used for *fire* is the same word for *fire* in John 18:18, where Peter and others warmed themselves on the night of Jesus' arrest and trial. It was the place of Peter's shame. I'm sure when Peter left the boat and made it to the shore dripping wet to the fire Jesus had made for him, that Peter recognized the smell of his shame—the burning wood.

As Peter stood at the fire and remembered how he couldn't stand with Jesus that evening when Jesus needed him most, Jesus served Peter and the other disciples breakfast. It was simple—fish and bread. It wasn't anything He prepared in advance or invested a lot of time preparing; it was what He had—no more and no less.

In the simplicity of their table on the beach, Jesus began discourse about love with Simon Peter. Jesus' answer to restoring Peter to a right relationship is seen in giving back. You see, Jesus knew that Peter loved Him. The *answer* to the "love" question wasn't what Jesus was looking for. Instead, He was looking for Peter to understand the message of giving back.

In other words, if someone invested in you and your life is changed, then you are called to invest in another. So, Jesus compelled Peter to feed, shepherd, and feed the sheep again. It's a reciprocal circle that continues to complete itself.

As we conclude *The Collective Journey*, let me ask you the question, "Will you feed, shepherd, and feed the sheep again?" If the answer is *yes*, then you belong to a tribe of mighty women right now, but your tribe is going to grow, so get ready.

My friend, continue to dream, but more importantly, pass on your dreams to the next generation. Have open palms, practice vulnerability and transparency, and release your dreams. Let me assure you that your dreams are safe with the coming generations because you have poured your life into their lives, and the tribal response is to protect the sacredness of your relationship and dreams. Because of the relationship, they anticipate the generational blessing of the passing on of dreams.

Lastly, keep preparing tables—small, large, medium-sized, tables on the sand, and beside still waters. Continue to prepare tables full of blessings, brokenness, and forgiveness.

As you are curled up in your chair with a cozy blanket, at the beach soaking up some sun, or sitting outside on the patio with your favorite drink, will you reflect one last time with me? Will you prayerfully ask God and yourself these questions and then wait to hear His still small voice speaking through you?

Reflection Questions:

1) What's your expansion plan?
2) How are you adding to your table?
3) Whom will you bring with you?

APPENDIX A: LIFE-GIVING ASSESSMENT

Life-Giving Is the Best Life

What are some ways that God gives life to you?

Check all that apply.

- ❏ Nature
- ❏ Exercise
- ❏ Long walks
- ❏ Hike
- ❏ Worship
- ❏ Spiritual friendships
- ❏ Shopping
- ❏ Self-care (manicure/pedicure, massage, etc.)
- ❏ Solitude
- ❏ Study
- ❏ Scripture
- ❏ Leading
- ❏ Art
- ❏ Rest
- ❏ Celebration
- ❏ Other:

- ❏ Recreation
- ❏ Family
- ❏ Long talks
- ❏ Laughter
- ❏ A cause/justice
- ❏ Volunteering
- ❏ Retreat
- ❏ Small group activities
- ❏ Game nights
- ❏ Hosting a dinner party
- ❏ Cooking/baking
- ❏ Gardening/yard work
- ❏ Decorating
- ❏ Organizing
- ❏ Reading

Living It Out—How can you incorporate these into your life?

APPENDIX B: THE SELF-DISCIPLINE OF SELF-CARE WORKSHEET

The Spiritual Discipline of Self-Care

Adele Ahlberg Calhoun, *Spiritual Disciplines Handbook: Practices That Transform Us.*

Reflection Questions:

1) God created you "very good." Thank God for making you.
    a. If you have a hard time thanking God for yourself, what does this reveal about how you value being made in His image?
2) Talk to God about what it is like to receive yourself as He receives you.
3) How have you neglected caring for your health, your body, your relationships?
4) How might Jesus be inviting you more deeply into some area of self-care?
5) What is experiencing burnout like for you? What do you do to recover?
6) How has it changed the way you live?
7) How might receiving yourself as a gift from God affect your life?
8) How do you protect yourself from receiving love from God and others?

Spiritual Exercises

1) Make a list of things you like about yourself.
2) Stand in front of the mirror and take a good look at your body.
    a. What does your body tell you about where you came from?
    b. What you have done in life? Your choices?

      c. Tell God how you react to what you see. What places of your past still need to be received and integrated into who you are?

3) Care for yourself by planning a day you would enjoy. Choose where you want to be and whom you want to be with. Celebrate the gift of the day and yourself.

4) Where in your body life do you need a new beginning?

      a. What practices and patterns that tie into food, sex, rest, work, or relationships would you like to change?

      b. How can you cooperate with God in an effort to honor your body as the temple of the Holy Spirit?

      c. Who can help you in this?

5) Sit quietly in a comfortable position. Breathe slowly and notice any tightness in your body. What is your body saying to you right now?

      a. How would Jesus want you to care for yourself right now?

6) Keep a record of how much sleep you are getting per night.

      a. Are you respecting your God-given need for rest and recreation?

      b. Readjust your sleeping or resting patterns for a week. What is it like for you?

7) Cultivate ways of nurturing and caring for your body: bubble baths, massages, exercise, soft sheets or pillows, buying some flowers, or reading a book. Spend time with your hobbies and people who bring life to you. Pick up an interest you left behind.

APPENDIX C: THE "I AM" SCRIPTURES

I am God's masterpiece. (Ephesians 2:10, Author paraphrased and amplified)
"For we are God's (own) handiwork (His workmanship), created in Christ Jesus, (born anew) that we may do those good works which God predestined for us (taking paths he planned for us ahead of time), that we should walk in them (living the good life which He prearranged and made ready for us to live.)"

I am forgiven. (Ephesians 1:7-8, CEB)
"We have been ransomed through His Son's blood, and we have forgiveness for our failures based on His overflowing grace, which He poured over us with wisdom and understanding."

I am a new creature. (2 Corinthians 5:17, CEB)
"So, then, if anyone is in Christ, that person is part of a new creation. The old things have gone away and look, new things have arrived."

I am strong in the Lord. (Ephesians 6:10, KJV)
"Finally my brethren, be strong in the Lord and in the power of His might."

I am accepted in Christ. (Ephesians 1:6, NKJV)
"To the praise of the glory of His grace, by which He made us accepted in the Beloved."

I am loved with an everlasting love. (Jeremiah 31:3, NKJV)
"The Lord has appeared of old to me saying: Yes, I have loved you with an everlasting love."

I am overtaken with blessings. (Deuteronomy 28:2-6, NKJV)
"And all these blessings shall come upon you and overtake you, because you obey the voice of the Lord your God. Blessed shall you be in the city, and blessed shall you be in the country. . . ." (And it goes on and on.)

APPENDIX D: A VISION AND VALUES STATEMENT EXAMPLE

The

Collective

j o u r n e y

EXAMPLE OF A PERSONAL VISION STATEMENT (LISA POTTER)

I remain a genuine grace-giver, a planting of the Lord who shines with the light of Jesus in all my relationships as a wife, mother, daughter, sister, aunt, friend, mentor, and motivator. Through relationships, writing, and speaking, I will turn my pain into passions and help others to do the same. I will allow God to use me in fresh and new ways as a bridge-builder for the generations coming after me.

Tag Line: A grace-giver, joy-bringer, bridge-builder, mentor, motivator, and planting of the Lord.

THIS PARAGRAPH IS OPTIONAL

It's important for me to include these words and concepts: genuine, grace, a tree or planting of the Lord, relationships, generations, and turning life's pain into passions. The idea of being genuine speaks of being real and authentic, displaying openness in a healing way. A giver of grace exemplifies someone who has received much grace and will also give grace greatly to the world and those whom God puts in my path. All of my life verses speak of a tree planted by waters and bearing much fruit in season: Psalm 1:3, Isaiah 61:3, Jeremiah 17:7-8. Family, friends, and relationships remain important to my health and peace. Those who come alongside to help me in tangible ways and provide encouragement give life to me as a person. I enjoy bridging the gap between the younger generations and turning my life's pain into passions to allow the Lord to use them to minister to others.

PERSONAL VALUES STATEMENT

- I will be planted. Isaiah 61:3 says, "And provide for those who grieve in Zion—to bestow on them a crown of beauty instead of ashes, the oil of joy instead of mourning, and a garment of praise instead of a spirit of despair. They will be called oaks of righteousness, a planting of the Lord for the display of his splendor."

- I will be a wife, mother, daughter, sister, aunt, mentor, writer, and speaker, investing and enriching the lives of those God puts in my path.

- I am invested in mentoring, making disciples, coaching spiritual daughters and sons, in the hope they will run further and faster, going places I will never go.

- I am carrying a sword as a war cry for the generation that is coming behind. Understanding what was and what is, and what God is going to do next.

- I will infuse new, fresh life where God has planted me.

- I will bring laughter and joy to the hurting and wounded.

- I will share what God has spoken to me through the tools of writing and speaking.

- I will allow my pain to birth passions in me. Always.

APPENDIX E: PERSONAL INVENTORY AND GROWTH PLAN

Personal Inventory and Growth Plan: Dates: _____

Spiritual	Physical	Family	Ministry	Sabbath/ Rest

APPENDIX F: THE RELATIONSHIP RESOURCE PAGE

MODELS
People who do what you'd like to do.

1. _____
2. _____
3. _____

HEROES
People you look up to and admire.

1. _____
2. _____
3. _____

MENTORS
People who coach you and invest in you.

1. _____
2. _____
3. _____

PARTNERS
*People who travel
with you and hold you accountable.*

1. _____
2. _____
3. _____

INNER CIRCLE
Those who are closest to you; they're like family.

1. _____
2. _____
3. _____

MENTEES
People who learn from you.

1. _____

2. _____

3. _____

"Evaluate your answers to the 'Your Network' diagram. Do you have a good balance of relationships that can be your emotional fuel? Which categories do you still need people to fill in your life: models, heroes, mentors, partners, inner circle, or followers? Jot down names of people you can challenge to be part of your network. List what role they can best fill for you.

"When you conclude what people still need to make up your network, go and meet with them. Challenge them to play a key role in your network. Invite them to play a bigger role, as a mentor, or partner, or model, or hero, or inner circle. Set times to meet with these people once a month for support, accountability, encouragement, and direction. Invite them to ask these questions of you:

- What are the goals you are working toward right now?
- How can I offer direction?
- In what ways can I hold you accountable?
- What are your greatest needs? Temptations? Weaknesses?
- What action step can you take this week? When will you take it?"[67]

---

67 Elmore and Herman, *Habitudes,* 18.

SOURCES CONSULTED

Ashbrook, R. Thomas. *Mansions of the Heart: Exploring Seven Stages of Spiritual Growth*. San Francisco: Jossey-Bass, 2009.

Barsh, Joanna, and Susie Cranston. *How Remarkable Women Lead: The Breakthrough Model for Work and Life*. New York: Crown Business, 2009.

Barton, Ruth Haley. *Strengthening the Soul of Your Leadership: Seeking God in the Crucible of Ministry*. Downers Grove, IL: InterVarsity Press, 2008.

Beach, Nancy. *Gifted to Lead: The Art of Leading as a Woman in the Church*. Grand Rapids, MI: Zondervan, 2008.

Blanchard, Ken, Phil Hodges, and Phyllis Hendry. *Lead Like Jesus Revisited: Lessons from the Greatest Leadership Role Model of All Time*. Nashville: Thomas Nelson, 2016.

Bradford, James T. *Lead So Others Can Follow*. Springfield, MO: Salubris Resources, 2015.

Bradley, Ian. *The Celtic Way*. London: Darton, Longman and Todd, 1993.

Brown, Brené. *The Gifts of Imperfection: Let Go of Who You Think You're Supposed to Be and Embrace Who You Are*. Center City, MN: Hazelden Publishing, 2010.

———. *Braving the Wilderness: The Quest for True Belonging and the Courage to Stand Alone*. New York: Random House, 2017.

Catron, Jenni. *The 4 Dimensions of Extraordinary Leadership: The Power of Leading from Your Heart, Soul, Mind, and Strength*. Nashville, TN: Thomas Nelson, 2015.

Calhoun, Adele Ahlberg. *Spiritual Disciplines Handbook: Practices That Transform Us*. Downers Grove, IL: InterVarsity Press, 2005.

Caliguire, Mindy. *Spiritual Friendship*. Downers Grove, IL: InterVarsity Press, 2007.

Charan, Ram, Steve Drotter, and Jim Noel. *The Leadership Pipeline: How to Build the Leadership Powered Company*. 2nd ed. San Francisco: Jossey-Bass, 2011.

Chole, Alicia Britt. *Anonymous: Jesus' Hidden Years and Yours*. Nashville, TN: Thomas Nelson, 2006.

———. *Ready Set Rest, The Practice of Prayer Retreating*. Rogersville, MO: Onewholeworld, 2014.

———. "Movement Two: Toward Intentionality, Week Eight," *The 7th Year*. March 16, 2015, www.the7thyear.com.

Clinton, J. Robert. *The Making of a Leader: Recognizing the Lessons and Stages of Leadership Development*. 2nd ed. Colorado Springs: NavPress, 2012.

Covey, Stephen. "The Law of the Farm." *Upprevention*. https://upprevention.org/the/34154-the-law-of-the-farm-by-stephen-covey-714-141.php.

DeGroat, Chuck. *Wholeheartedness: Busyness, Exhaustion, and Healing the Divided Self.* Grand Rapids, MI: Wm. B. Eerdmans Publishing Co., 2016.

Elmore, Tim, and Harvey Herman. *Habitudes: Images That Form Leadership Habits and Attitudes.* Atlanta: Growing Leaders, Inc., 2013.

Goldsmith, Malcolm. *Knowing Me, Knowing God: Exploring Your Spirituality with Myers-Briggs.* Nashville: Abingdon Press, 1997.

Jones, Timothy. *Finding a Spiritual Friend: How Friends and Mentors Can Make Your Faith Grow.* Nashville, TN: Upper Room Books, 1998.

KPMG. "Moving Women Forward into Leadership Roles." *Women's Leadership Study.* https://home.kpmg/content/dam/kpmg/ph/pdf/ThoughtLeadershipPublications/ KPMGWomensLeadershipStudy.pdf.

Kreider, Larry. *The Cry for Spiritual Fathers & Mothers.* Lititz, PA: House to House Publications, 2000.

Magee, Jeffery. *The Managerial Leadership Bible: Learning the Strategic, Organizational, and Tactical Skills Everyone Needs Today.* Upper Saddle River, NJ: Pearson Education, Inc., 2015.

Manning, Brennan, and Jim Hancock. *Posers, Fakers, & Wannabes: Unmasking the Real You.* Colorado Springs, CO: NavPress, 2003.

McGee, Robert S. *The Search for Significance: Seeing Your True Worth through God's Eyes.* Nashville, TN: Thomas Nelson Publishers, 2003.

McIntosh, Gary L., and Samuel D. Rima, Sr. *Overcoming the Dark Side of Leadership: The Paradox of Personal Dysfunction.* Grand Rapids, MI: Baker Books, 1997.

McKay, Lisa. *You Can Still Wear Cute Shoes.* Colorado Springs: CO: David C. Cook, 2010.

McNeal, Reggie. *A Work of Heart: Understanding How God Shapes Spiritual Leaders.* San Francisco: Jossey-Bass, 2011.

Metaxas, Eric. *7 Women and the Secret of Their Greatness.* Nashville: Thomas Nelson, 2015.

Miller, Hodde, Sharon. "What Happens When We See Women Teach the Bible." *Christianity Today.* http://www.christianitytoday.com/women/2015/january/what-happens-when-we-see-wome n-teach-bible.html.

Nessa, Lynn. "A Lesson from the Myrtle Tree." *Inspirational Contemplation.* https://nessalynn77. wordpress.com/2011/02/12/a-lesson-from-the-myrtle-tree/.

Nouwen, Henri J. M. *Life of the Beloved.* New York: Crossroad, 1992.

O'Dea, Lori. "Is Leadership a Gender-Neutral Issue?" *Influence Magazine*, August-September 2015.

Ortberg, John. *The Me I Want to Be: Becoming God's Best Version of You.* Grand Rapids, MI: Zondervan, 2010.

———. *Soul Keeping: Caring for the Most Important Part of You.* Grand Rapids, MI: Zondervan, 2014.

Palmer, Parker J. *A Hidden Wholeness: Toward an Undivided Life.* San Francisco: Jossey-Bass, 2004.

Platt, David. *Follow Me: A Call to Die. A Call to Live.* Carol Stream, IL: Tyndale House Publishers, Inc., 2013.

Reese, Randy D., and Robert Loane. *Deep Mentoring: Guiding Others on Their Leadership Journey.* Downers Grove, IL: InterVarsity Press, 2012.

Sandberg, Sheryl. *Lean In: Women, Work, and the Will to Lead.* New York: Alfred A. Knopf, 2013.

Seamands, David A. *Healing for Damaged Emotions: Recovering from the Memories That Cause Our Pain.* Wheaton, IL: Victor Books, 1991.

Scazzero, Peter. *Emotionally Healthy Spirituality: It's Impossible to Be Spiritually Mature While Remaining Emotionally Immature.* Grand Rapids, IL: Zondervan, 2006.

Scott, Halee Gray. *Dare Mighty Things.* Grand Rapids, MI: Zondervan, 2014

Smedes, Lewis B. *Shame and Grace: Healing the Shame We Don't Deserve.* New York: Harper Collins Publishing, 1993.

———. *Forgive and Forget: Healing the Hurts We Don't Deserve.* San Francisco: Harper Collins, 1996.

Smith, Gordon T. *Courage and Calling: Embracing Your God-Given Potential.* Downers Grove, IL: InterVarsity Press, 2011.

Tennant, Carolyn. *Catch the Wind of the Spirit: How the 5 Ministry Gifts Can Transform Your Church.* Springfield, MO: Vital Resources, 2016.

Thompson, Curt. *The Anatomy of the Soul: Surprising Connections between Neuroscience and Spiritual Practices That Can Transform Your Life and Relationships.* Carol Stream, IL: Tyndale, 2010.

———. *The Soul of Shame: Retelling the Stories We Believe about Ourselves.* Downers Grove, IL: InterVarsity Press, 2015.

Voskamp, Ann. *The Greatest Gift, Unwrapping the Full Love Story of Christmas.* Carol Stream, IL: Tyndale, 2013.

Weems, Kerri. *Rhythms of Grace.* Grand Rapids, MI: Zondervan, 2014.

Willard, Dallas. *Renovation of the Heart: Putting on the Character of Christ.* Colorado Springs, CO: NavPress, 2012.

———. *The Spirit of the Disciplines: Understanding How God Changes Lives.* New York: Harper Collins Publishers, 1988.